Australian Biographical Monographs

24

Australian Biographical Monographs

Series Editor: Scott Prasser

Previous Volumes

Henry Bolte	Megan Murphy
Rex Patterson	Lyndon Megarrity
Brian Harradine	Keith Harvey
Arthur Calwell	James Franklin and Gerry ONolan
Joseph Cook	Zachary Gorman
Annabelle Rankin	Peter Sekuless
Robert (Bob) Hawke	Mike Steketee
John Curtin	David Lee
Jack Lang	David Clune
Leonie Kramer	Damien Freeman
Margaret Guilfoyle	Anne Henderson
William McKell	David Clune
Neville Bonner	Sean Jacobs
George Reid	Luke Walker
Robert Askin	Paul Loughnan
John Grey Gorton	Paul Williams
Stanley Melbourne Bruce	David Lee
Robert Menzies	Scott Prasser
Neville Wran	David Clune
Lindsay Thompson	William Westerman
Johannes Bjelke-Petersen	Bruce Kingston
Harold Holt	Tom Frame
Joseph Lyons	Kevin Andrews

Australian Biographical Monographs

24

James Scullin

Michael Easson

Connor Court Publishing

Australian Biographical Monographs 24
James Scullin by Michael Easson
Published in 2024 by Connor Court Publishing Pty Ltd

Copyright © Michael Easson

All rights reserved. No part of this book may be reproduced or transmitted in any form or by any means, electronic or mechanical, including photo copying, recording or by any information storage and retrieval system, without prior permission in writing from the publisher.

Connor Court Publishing Pty Ltd
PO Box 7257
Redland Bay QLD 4165
sales@connorcourt.com
www.connorcourt.com

Printed in Australia

ISBN: 9781923224384

Front Cover Photograph: James Scullin. Taken between 1929 and 1932. Source: http://nla.gov.au/nla.obj-136264498, National Library of Australia.

In memory of Don Rawson (1930-1997) and for Race Mathews (1935-) who planned his next book would be on Scullin

Prime Minister James Scullin and wife Sarah, October 1929, Photo: News Ltd/Newspix, from the Museum of Australian Democracy archives.

Series overview

The Connor Court Publishing's ***Australian Biographical Series*** on past leading Australian political leaders and other important figures seeks to provide an overview for those who are unfamiliar with the subject and to highlight the person's particular importance, controversies and contributions to Australia's progress.

The monographs are scholarly rather than academic in focus placing emphasis on a clear narrative, but with careful attention to referencing to ensure views expressed are supported by appropriate sources and evidence.

The Series was initiated because of the decline in the study of Australian history at our schools and universities and the consequential lack of knowledge or even worse, distorted views of some of Australia's leading figures who deserve to be remembered, understood for both their achievements, and as each volume also highlights, their flaws.

This volume focusses on James Scullin, Labor Prime Minister from 1929-32, Australia's first Prime Minister of Catholic faith, which profoundly influenced him, though he saw secular and religious principles as compatible rather than competing. The last full biography on Scullin was in 1974, so it is timely that this new monograph has been done as his place in Australian Government has tended to become overlooked. This new monograph by Michael Easson highlights the many policy and political challenges that Scullin faced – the Great Depression, Labor Party factionalism and betrayal, and the need to deal with strong and difficult personalities. Not lost though, is how Easson has conveyed that amid all these unrelenting pressures, was Scullin's intrinsic decency, sincerity, and humility. He kept it to the end. There is much to admire.

Michael Easson AM is a businessman, company director, former union leader and Labor historian of some note. He was Secretary of the Labor Council of NSW [now called Unions NSW], 1989-94; a Vice President of the Australian Council of Trade Unions, 1993-94; and Senior Vice President of the NSW ALP, 1993-95. He holds a MSc from Oxford University and PhDs from UNSW and the University of Melbourne.

- **Scott Prasser**

(Editor - Australian Biographical Monographs)

Author's Note

All biographical accounts of a former prime minister should be truth-seeking quests. What to include, the context of the time, the records worth consulting and drawing from, require judgement and perspective. In James Scullin's case, there is little of the directly personal to consult. His papers in the National Library of Australia almost entirely refer to his visit to the United Kingdom (UK) in 1930-31 on one issue – his efforts to persuade the King to appoint an Australian as Governor-General.

There are records in the national archives, other source material and memoirs, including the papers of Catholic intellectual and Labor sympathiser Kevin Kelly,[1] whom Scullin first knew in Ballarat. There are also newspapers and recollections and assessments in books and essays. Scullin's 27 months as Australian Prime Minister, 1929-1932, the wrecking trauma of those years, the Great Depression crises, were once as closely examined by contemporary writers and historians as anything else in Australia's history. Scullin the tragic, unlucky failure was a common refrain about his brief prime ministership. Yet political good fortune once smiled upon him. As Richard Crossman, UK Cabinet Minister in the Labour governments of Harold Wilson, once remarked in his diaries, in politics "where there's death, there's hope."[2] Scullin was lucky that Labor Leader Frank Tudor died in 1922, as after a by-election Scullin inherited the safe seat of Yarra in the Federal Parliament. Five years later, Anstey was unwell and resigned the deputy leadership of the Labor

Party. Scullin, who had acquired a reputation for mastery of fiscal and tax issues, won the ballot as his replacement. One year later, after Federal Leader Matthew Charlton's health broke down, on 26 April 1928 Scullin was elected Leader. Fate, the cards falling nicely, what could go wrong? Nearly seven months after winning the leadership, Scullin lost the 17 November 1928 election. Then, after colossal miscalculations by the then Prime Minister Stanley Melbourne Bruce, a new election was called for 12 October 1929 with victory for Scullin and the Labor team. Then came the crisis for which there could be no preparation. Labor intellectual and MHR Kim. E. Beazley,[3] once asked Scullin if he would write his memoirs. He replied simply: "[The Great Depression] nearly killed me to live through it. It would kill me to write about it."[4]

Don Rawson[5] (1930-1997), a political scientist, wrote about Labor politics in the 1930s and told me what he thought about that history. Forty years later, I have had to freshly think about the troubled Labor prime minister he knew.

In searching for direction, guidance, and inspiration, this monograph suggests a truth: road maps to a politician's life sometimes seem imprinted with disappearing ink. So much is feint or missing. Yet two books, John Robertson's biography *J.H. Scullin*[6] and Liam Byrne's *Becoming John Curtin and James Scullin*,[7] help light a path to understanding a now distant period and a life. From fragments of recorded memory, archival material, and assessments of others, what seems true, fair, and persuasive to this author is now presented.

That is the objective of this brief work: To discover the Scullin who never hid from view.

In reaching my assessment, I am grateful to David Clune and Damian Grace for reading and commenting on an earlier draft. Jeff Kildea helped explain the Victorian State 'Scripture Referendum' of 1904. All errors, 'clangers' of misinterpretation, and other deserved pillories, are entirely mine.

Finally, I express my thanks to Ann Kelly and Dr Barbara Cooper for access to their father's (K.T. Kelly) papers at the National Library of Australia. Librarians and archivists at the State Library of Victoria, the Queensland State Library, and the NLA answered various research inquiries. I am grateful to the Trove, NLA for the digitalisation of Australian newspapers and magazines which has been of immeasurable assistance to historians like me.

Scullin sits for a portrait Mr William Beckwith McInnes, the Melbourne artist, who has been commissioned by the Commonwealth Government for the work. Sydney Morning Herald, 22 July 1937, p. 10.

Introduction

There is a revealing line about James Scullin published in in 1966 by Beazley: "Denounced in [the 1930s by] the NSW Labor movement, especially as a conservative, he had a[n earlier] career of sponsorship of revolutionary and militant proposals in the Federal Conferences of the Australian Labor Party (ALP)."[8] Scullin, early school leaver, jack-of-all-trades turned grocer, journalist, Australian Workers' Union (AWU) organiser and politician, pious and devout Catholic, is more of a puzzle than might be expected. Bewildered and politically devoured by the economic and sociopolitical turmoil of the Great Depression, Prime Minister 1929-1932, Leader of the Labor Party, 1928 to 1935, Leader of the Opposition in 1928 and again from 1932-1935, Member of the House of Representatives from 1910-1913, and again from 1922 to 1949, Scullin was decried as "the man who failed, even at failure."[9] By those words was meant not failure whilst defying the odds, failure in "daring greatly" in Theodore Roosevelt's oft quoted panegyric,[0] but clueless, compass-less failure to forge direction and inspiration in the defining moments of his career. During his prime ministership there were moments of inspiration, crypto-Keynesian insights, followed by anti-growth conservative policies to cut wages and pensions, and other initiatives which depressed and demoralised supporters.

Scullin was sworn in as prime minister in the week of the Wall Street Crash, October 1929. In Scullin's defence, no world leader shone brilliant in the immediacy that followed the emergence of the Great Depression, its consequent economic decay, and massive, rising unemployment. All prime ministers, presidents, and world leaders were unsure what to do.

Whitlam once argued the case for Scullin:

> It is the convention to regard J.H. Scullin as a mere orator who found himself thrust into an economic catastrophe completely beyond him and who let Australia and his party just drift deeper into disaster. This is of course true in the sense that no leader in the world was found adequate to cope nationally or internationally with the Depression; but no nation was more at the mercy of international decisions than Australia. In no country were the great financial interests more selfish or more remote. No leader had to deal with such turbulent and doubtful supporters. None had to deal with so unrelenting and unpatriotic an opposition as that which the Nationalist majority in the Senate provided. None had to operate within such an intractable federal system and deal with so formidable a manipulator of the system's contradictions as Lang was.[11]

Whitlam only touches on the complexities Scullin faced. It was even more complicated – as this monograph explains and evaluates. Importantly, there was another achievement: Scullin helped to block Jack Lang's takeover of the ALP and the ushering of Peronismo-type government.[12] That is, – strong man front, government by personality cult, rabble rousing, authoritarian dominance over party and state. Admittedly, unlike Juan Peron, the dictator of Argentina, 1946-55, the NSW Labor Leader was only a state boss and did not have an army at his disposal. The analogy can only be stretched too far and at the risk of distraction in a work on Scullin.[13] But it is worth noting how bad Lang was. The man, the "human thundercloud" in Bede Nairn's words, NSW Labor Leader, 1923-1939, Premier, 1925-27 and 1930-32, "simply tried to trample on those who opposed him... As a politician he achieved very little... his attempts to control the Depression were reckless and finally disastrous."[14] Preventing Lang from seizing control of national Labor was a formidable accomplishment.

Back to Beazley's point: Quizzically, what the early 1930s revealed as the cautious, hesitant Scullin belied his earlier years as a confident, radical activist about much of what the Labor Party debated, resolved, and stood for. The evolution of Scullin over time, from radical Laborite to moderate Labor leader, elder statesman and mentor, is not a hollow Russian Doll theme of mystery after perplexing mystery. His whole life was a battle, personal and public, to reconcile his faiths in his church and in the labour movement. His leadership was a constant encounter with the tests and tribulations that came with striving for social justice against complacent laissez-faire capitalism.

Scullin was the first Irish Catholic Australian to lead his party and his nation, only the second man to win office for Labor from the conservatives at a national election between 1901 and 1972. (The first was Andrew Fisher, who won elections outright in 1910 and 1914. Fisher was defeated in-between time, in 1913, losing to Joseph Cook.) Scullin was the only Labor prime minister elected from Victoria between 1901 and Hawke's election in 1983. (Though, of course, Curtin was born in Victoria and spent his formative years there, only moving to Western Australia in 1917, age 32.) Scullin swept to power at elections on 12 October 1929 winning by the greatest margin ever. He lost by the greatest margin ever for the Labor Party when his party – split, divided, and broken – faced the people again on 19 December 1931. Scullin, who seemed perceptive, clever, and considered about Australia's main economic challenges on the eve of obtaining government, crumbled during his period in office. Former Tasmanian Labor Premier Joe Lyons who was urged in 1929 by Scullin to resign as state Labor Leader and (successfully) contest Wilmot for Labor in the Federal Parliament, at first served as Postmaster-General and Works and Railways Minister in Scullin's government and, while Scullin was overseas, August 1930 to January 1931, as Acting Treasurer. Then, on Scullin's return he reappointed Ted Theodore as Treasurer. As a consequence, Lyons resigned from the ministry as well as the Labor Party, and began the formation of an anti-Labor coalition, the All For Australia League,[15] formed from ALP defectors and dissident Nationalists, which had much grass roots support and was initially anti-political party in its ideology. Lyons saw the opportunity to replace the Nationalists and most of the latter together with his supporters coalesced into the United Australia Party (UAP). On 7 May 1931, Lyons announced that as Leader of the UAP, the largest party opposed to the government, he was now Leader of the Opposition. John Latham, the last Nationalist Leader, and prior Leader of the Opposition, was his Deputy. Latham had stood aside for Lyons. On another flank, the Langites, followers of NSW Labor leader and demagogue Jack Lang, advocate of repudiation of government international loan borrowings, fiercely criticised Scullin. In early March 1931, the leader of the Lang grouping in the Federal Labor caucus, Jack Beasley,[16] resigned from the government. This followed a ballot for a new Ministry in March. Beasley missed out and thereafter took five other supporters with him away from the government benches. On 27 March the NSW party broke away from Federal Labor, forming 'NSW Labor' as a distinct party. Calling on Scullin to resign, Beasley who would thereafter be known as "stabber Jack" Beasley, led the Lang group of MPs to support a motion of no confidence in the Scullin Government, which succeeded on 25 November 1931. A year after his sensational defection from Labor, on 6 January 1932 Joe Lyons was sworn in as prime minister, after leading the UAP to a big election win.

Labor and the nation were divided by the Premiers' Plan and other ideas for taking Australia out of the Depression. It was not a simple battle of a few plans. The Premiers' Plan adopted at a Conference of the Prime Minister, Federal Treasurer, and State Premiers, in June 1931 was one of many reactions and programs for dealing with the crisis. It was shifting warfare, with positions espoused in Cabinet and Caucus porous to reinterpretation, amendment, and complete change, depending on arguments, criticisms, fear, political feedback, and threats. Earlier, the Melbourne Agreement of August 1930 between the Commonwealth and State Leaders required all state and Commonwealth Budgets be balanced in the 1930-31 financial year and those following. The month before, 17 July, Ted Theodore stepped down from Cabinet. Scullin left Australia at the end of August 1930, with ministers (and friends) Frank Brennan and Parker Moloney. In the intervening period, from August to return in January 1931, then the debates leading to the Premiers' Plan, was a roiling period of controversy and bitter debate.[17] Peter Cook argues comprehensively in his study of the government, just how much the government was in turmoil. In Warren Denning's account of the Scullin Government, he says the "party was in a state of drifting chaos".[18]

On Labor's far Left, the Communist Party, its ring leaders chosen by the Comintern, was resurgent in many trade unions, sparking strike action and inviting merciless critiques of 'do nothing Labor'. It was an era of sloganising and ideological peddling by extremes who declared they had 'the answer'. Even some of Labor's usually more perceptive voices were saying the honourable course was to resign office,[19] and let the other side lose credibility by governing – as if surrendering the Treasury benches was sensible, worthy, brave, and/or good for Labor and its supporters. Curtin was one who argued: "The proper course is to resign, rather than stultify the movement and be dishonoured for a generation."[20]

In the early 1930s, everybody was a politician, everybody a critic, everyone an adherent of some financial creed or another. Numerous plans and associated prescriptions for dealing with the crisis abounded – all subject to amendments and revisions, all products of anxiety about the grim fact of unemployment and the inability of the 'system' to provide work. The obvious helplessness of the Federal Government to apply credit policy independent of the sanction of the Commonwealth Bank Board contributed to uncertainty and the sense of crisis. The government itself was torn and divided, changing tack, reversing agreed positions, desperately responding to 'events'.

Defeated in late 1931, Scullin remained in the national parliament another 18 years. In that period, he came to be regarded by his Labor peers as a stateman who had lived the whole history of Australian Labor in the Commonwealth, its triumphs, splits, tragedies, and disasters, who yet seemed serenely unembittered.

Who was the paradox that was Scullin? This monograph answers the question and forms a conclusion: Scullin tasted failure, but he was never a failure himself.

The Evolution of a Labor Activist

James Scullin was born on 18 September 1876, the middle of nine children of Irish immigrants John Scullin, rail worker, and Ann, née Logan, domestic duties, both of whom came from County Derry in Ireland. After arriving in Australia in 1862, John Scullin at first worked as a farm labourer, saving enough money to bring his bride-to-be to Australia. They were married at St. Alipius Catholic Church, Ballarat, 25 January 1868.

Schooled at Trawalla, Victoria, then the Mount Rowan school near Ballarat, young Scullin grew up in the days of flickering lantern slide presentations, a time before the beginnings of cinema. If we were capable of piecing together his life, we might find an image of an isolated homestead where he grew up. A sister recalled that they never saw another child until they walked to school.[21] The children fished for yabbies and eels at a creek a quarter of a mile away. They set snares for rabbits. Another scene would show Scullin learning the violin, leaving school at age 14 to work in a grocer's shop in Ballarat. A fan of Victorian football, his career as a player was brief. He was never in robust health after a childhood accident. One day at school he and other boys were playing leapfrog. The young Scullin was not quite ready as one child crashed onto his back.[22] He spent six months in hospital, including his 10th birthday, in plaster. He read all the Dickens' novels in convalescence.

A frequent visitor to the Ballarat Library, Scullin met James Vallance, the Librarian who was an adjudicator in Ballarat's

South Street Society and at their annual Australasian Eisteddfod.[23] A member of the St Patrick's Debating Society and participant in the South Street Society, Scullin was said to be one of the best debaters of his time in those training schools of oratory.[24]

Debate and discussion within the Australian labour movement, local debating societies, and the Australian Natives Association, were James Scullin's higher education. He won debates and became an adjudicator at competitions. Scullin combined pride in his Irish ancestry and love for the poetical works of Scotsman Robbie Burns. Widely read, curious and inquiring, Scullin the autodidact exemplified the dynamic, educative creativity available to an enterprising colonial bent on self-improvement. A person of plain tastes, it was porridge and toast in the morning, and simple fare at the table. A dedicated teetotaller, he never drew a cigarette, puffed a cigar, or soothed his nerves with a pipe. A shot of wavy hair, flicked over his forehead, completed the picture of a cartoonist's dream subject.

As depression gripped country Victoria during the 1890s, Scullin picked up any job he could, including labouring work in mines and on farms. After exhausting workdays, he could be frequently found studying at evening classes, in public libraries, or reading at home – with illumination from candles and oil lamps. On 11 November 1907 at St Patrick's Cathedral, Ballarat, he married Sarah Maria McNamara, dressmaker, the daughter of a local AWU official. Another scene would show him chatting to his parish priest about Pope Leo XIII's (1891) encyclical

Rerum Novarum on what were the rights and duties of capital and labour and the implications for seeking social justice in the world. A young Scullin would have stirred to read the ringing, opening passages of the Church's clarion call:

> 2. ...venerable brethren, as on former occasions when it seemed opportune to refute false teaching, We have addressed you in the interests of the Church and of the common weal, and have issued letters bearing on political power, human liberty, the Christian constitution of the State, and like matters, so have We thought it expedient now to speak on the condition of the working classes. ... The discussion is not easy, nor is it void of danger. It is no easy matter to define the relative rights and mutual duties of the rich and of the poor, of capital and of labour. And the danger lies in this, that crafty agitators are intent on making use of these differences of opinion to pervert men's judgments and to stir up the people to revolt.

> 3. In any case we clearly see, and on this there is general agreement, that some opportune remedy must be found quickly for the misery and wretchedness pressing so unjustly on the majority of the working class: for the ancient workingmen's guilds were abolished in the last century, and no other protective organisation took their place. Public institutions and the laws set aside the ancient religion. Hence, by degrees it has come to pass that

> working men have been surrendered, isolated and helpless, to the hard-heartedness of employers and the greed of unchecked competition. The mischief has been increased by rapacious usury, which, although more than once condemned by the Church, is nevertheless, under a different guise, but with like injustice, still practiced by covetous and grasping men. To this must be added that the hiring of labour and the conduct of trade are concentrated in the hands of comparatively few; so that a small number of very rich men have been able to lay upon the teeming masses of the labouring poor a yoke little better than that of slavery itself.

Those last words were not mere analysis. They were an exhortation to do something.

The encyclical supported trade union organisation and denounced extreme socialist – and Communist doctrines – of expropriating all private property. And condemned the surrender to the state of the sphere of private liberty and conscience. Although the Church attacked the virtual serfdom of wage earners under unbridled capitalism, there was messy ambiguity as to what else to do. Interestingly, Kevin Kelly in reviewing Robertson's life of Scullin recognised that the encyclical "threw no light on the modalities of workers' ownership of large-scale enterprises,"[25] and other issues. The faithful had to find their own way to solutions that might work.

The image burns strong, more than 120 years later, of Scullin, active in the study groups of the Catholic Young

Men's Society, asking about what this injunction to the faithful from the leader of his Church meant in practical terms. "I wouldn't worry about it, son" is unlikely to have been in the top rank of responses Scullin expected from his spiritual mentor the day he asked. Australian historian of church and state, John Molony unmasks the culprit:

> Many years ago, Bishop Basil Roper[26] told me a story of an event in his life which he much regretted. Before the First World War he was a young priest at the cathedral presbytery in Ballarat… One day, he was called to the parlour where a young man awaited him with a small document in his hand. It was a copy of *Rerum Novarum,* and the young man wanted the priest to explain its contents to him. The priest was forced to tell him that he could not do so because, although he was aware of Leo's encyclical, he was unable to explain it as he had never studied it. The young man went away unsatisfied and, according to the bishop, ceased from that day to interest himself in the social teachings of the Church to which he belonged. It was regrettable because he was James Scullin…[27]

Born in Warrnambool, Roper was ordained in Sydney in late November 1911 and was then posted to Ballarat. This conversation, then, must have been after Scullin's active involvement in the Labor Party, Catholic and other debating circles, and when Scullin was an MHR. The gist of the conversation may be true, but not that Scullin took Roper's response as a credible answer. Roper's ignorance then of Pope Leo's thought was apparently matched by his subsequent lack of appreciation of the evolution of Scullin's religious and political views, assuming the accuracy of Molony's account. Scullin was not deterred by this recently ordained priest, brilliantly schooled in scholasticism, too busy to think about recent Catholic social justice theory. Molony claims "Scullin's knowledge of Catholic social teaching was minimal and had no appreciable effect on his consciousness."[28] This misconstrues the evidence.[29] On the contrary, Jim Franklin argues: "James Scullin ... [was] close to [Melbourne Archbishop] Mannix over *Rerum Novarum* while warning him of the dangers of a separatist Catholic party."[30] Race Mathews explains that Scullin's curiosity about the issues was far from cursory:

> Scullin's interest in the Church's social teachings was undeterred. The enlightenment that he had been denied at the presbytery door was pursued instead through widespread reading that included the Distributist weeklies, the *Eye Witness*[31] and the *New Witness*.[32] Articles by Belloc were reprinted in the Ballarat newspaper, the *Ballarat Echo*, which he edited from 1913 until 1922, and his biographer sees the encyclical as having influenced him on questions of social justice.[33]

Belloc's influence is further discussed below.

Scullin's political evolution is worth considering. He joined the Labor Party in 1903, or more accurately, the recently formed Political Labor Council (PLC), which became the local Labor Party branch. Scullin was apparently inspired by the British socialist-agitator Tom Mann, who did much in 1903 to inspire the organisation of country branches of political Labor, as well as union organising, after whirlwind visits across the state. Mann's visit to Ballarat was the impetus to form the PLC branch,[34] which Scullin joined.[35] Labor was a party which "was a network of people who dreamed and laboured and plotted to realise social change."[36] As an early recruit in the district to Labor and radicalism, Scullin pondered, self-educated himself, discussed and debated, what he should do. The urgent injunction for Scullin was to seek truth and justice in daily life, to give witness to the Christian Gospel through applying the teachings of Jesus to the here and now. There was enough distress, penury, hardship, and injustice locally, around him, to stir Scullin into action.

In 1906, three years after joining, Scullin won Labor selection by a substantial margin to stand against the Prime Minister, Alfred Deakin, the then Federal Member for Ballaarat, as the electorate was then called.[37] The "unknown little grocer's assistant", one report said, would "…oppose our great Prime Minister."[38] A profile on Scullin attested to his determination: "He knows what hard graft is, having worked as a battery boy, wood chopper, tributer in mines, navvy, etc., and is now the proprietor of a flourishing grocery business in Skipton-street, Ballarat. As a child of ten he met with a severe accident to his spine, and invalided for some years, he gave himself up to serious study."[39] Joseph W. Kirton[40] nominated for the Anti-Socialists: "Mr. Kirton's candidature… encouraged the [Labor] Party to believe that with a split anti-socialist vote they would win. Then came Mr. Kirton's withdrawal, and herein lies the hope of Mr. Deakin's supporters."[41] With Reid's old Free Trade Party re-branded the Anti-Socialist Party, with Deakin's Protectionists fearing that the rising Labor vote might erode their electoral prospects, anything was possible in the seat and the nation. The previous Federal election in 1903 saw three parties, the Free Traders, Protectionists, and Labor, evenly divided. Deakin quipped it was like 'three elevens' on the field. The 'match' ideally required just two teams, he implied. National elections between 1901 and 1918 were fought on the first-past-the-post basis. If the non-Labor parties were evenly split in Ballarat and Labor got above a third of the vote, Scullin had a chance.

Kirton,[42] was a formidable foe, the former state MLA for Ballarat West, 1889-1904, an able debater, liberal in many of his views, and not a predictable, conservative Free Trader. His nomination was tactical. A report claimed: "It was no secret in Ballarat that Mr. Kirton's nomination was engineered from Melbourne and Sydney. The remnant of the old Victorian Free Trade Party, with its rich Freetrade backing, supplied the moving spirits."[43] The AWU mouthpiece, *The Worker*, claimed: "The withdrawal of Joseph Kirton at the last moment – so that nobody else could be nominated – was practically engineered by that doughty political masquerader Alexander Peacock,[44] but there are a number of Anti Soshites[45] very sore over the business."[46] Kirton pledged support for Deakin in the battle ahead.

On 23 October 1906, on a wet night, risen from his sick bed with the 'flu, Scullin spoke to a crowd gathered in Her Majesty's Theatre, Ballarat. The rapturous report in *The Worker* read:

> Speaking with a fine fluency of phrase, a clear reasoning grasp of the Federal politics of the day, and a searching criticism of the actions of the Prime Minister, Mr. Scullin had his audience in rapt attention. Nothing he set out to explain was misunderstood. It was an exposition of the aims of Labor which the oldest warhorse of the party might have been proud to claim his own. On the destructive side, he penetrated the woeful weaknesses of the anti-Labor parties with the keenness of a needle on a professional mission.[47]

Interestingly, Watson, the Federal Parliamentary Labor Leader, was reluctant to support Scullin. Visiting UK Labour Leader Ramsay MacDonald spoke for Scullin on the stump, but Watson was nowhere to be seen in Ballarat.[48] Watson was hopeful of a Liberal-Labor alliance, led by Deakin. Indeed, after the 1906 election, an informal coalition of Deakin's Protectionists and Labor's MHRs, with Deakin as PM, was kept in office. Andrew Fisher, after Watson vacated the leadership of Labor in 1907, continued to support Deakin, but then swapped roles, becoming Prime Minister with Deakin's support in 1908.

In the eventuality, however, in Ballaarat on 12 December 1906, Scullin scored 33.8 per cent of the vote, Deakin 66.2 per cent. At the declaration of the poll, Prime Minister Deakin seemed both elated and annoyed, as he 'whistled' to his supporters that the result was fantastic, despite appearances and reality. Deakin said of his Protectionists: "Their party was the one which, in this election, was to be crushed out between the two others; there was to be nothing left of them at all. They went into the fight without funds, and subject to a considerable amount of calumny; yet in spite of all the forces arrayed against them, they had held their own..."[49] Except they had not. The Protectionists lost 10 seats compared to 1903. The 1906 result was 16 Protectionists, 4 Independent Protectionists, 26 Labor members and 27 Anti-Socialists (formerly George Reid's Free Traders). The other 2 seats were won by a Western Australia party. Labor almost exactly matched Reid's Anti-Socialists.

In 1907, there was speculation that Scullin might run for the state seat of Ballarat West,[50] held from 1904 by Henry Scott Bennett, also known as Henry Gilbert Bennett,[51] who decided not to stand again. But Scullin never sought preselection, perhaps thinking the manner of Scott Bennett's departure from politics (in sullen disillusion) would harm the Labor vote. Indeed, at the Victorian state elections in 1907, the Labor vote was a little less than 35 per cent, with Kirton winning his old seat back.

Running against Deakin meant Scullin got noticed. Appointed in 1908 an Organiser for the Australian Workers' Union, whose Victorian country branch was headquartered in Ballarat, Scullin recruited and organised. He regarded political Labor and unions as entwined. He set up branches of the Labor Party throughout western Victoria. Between February 1908 and February 1909, the number of affiliated

Labor branches in the country swelled from 43 to 96, the number of country members increased from 1880 to 5710. Frank Bongiorno in his study of Victorian Labor argues: "This was primarily the achievement of Scullin and the AWU."[52] As a union organiser, Scullin was involved in union and political agitation. For example, helping to set up a branch of the Carters' and Drivers' Industrial Union in Ballarat.[53] Robertson notes: "…for part of the next few years Scullin jogged with horse and buggy along rough roads winding through the green, pleasant countryside of his beloved Victoria…"[54] A contemporary ALP report noted: "In the country districts members of the state and Federal Labor parties rendered invaluable assistance, but to the Australian Workers' Union it is due to say that its political organiser, Mr. J.H. Scullin was the greatest force in advocating the Labor platform."[55] Scullin considered himself a socialist. But then – more than in later years – socialism was "a diverse field of multiple perspectives".[56]

Scullin in this period knew of John Curtin, who had grown up in Creswick, 18.5km from Ballarat, but moved to Melbourne as a young child. Curtin also heard and was inspired by Mann. Curtin joined the Victorian Socialist Party (VSP), which distinctively of the early socialist sects sought to win friends and influence within Labor, rather than in place of Labor. This was unlike, for example, the equivalent or comparable bodies in NSW, who in sectarian and determined isolation advocated the purity of separation from the House of Labor through fighting for 'real socialism' rather than 'milk and water' reformism.[57] In some ways, the VSP was like the British Independent

Labour Party,[58] a ginger group on the socialist left, wanting to shape and persuade Labor from within.[59]

Ironically, in NSW and Queensland where the Labor Party achieved early success, the doctrinaire socialists had greater sway with a bigger bulk of purists to talk to. In Victoria, the going was tougher, the state returning smaller percentages of MPs to state and national parliaments than in NSW or Queensland. For this, Don Rawson attributes the lack of a rural base, including metal-mining in the state, as a major factor.[60] In the first decade after federation, progressive liberalism captured the imagination in Victoria. Labor governments were formed nationally in 1910, in NSW and South Australia in the same year, whereas the Victorians waited until 1952 to win outright. And three years later, after a catastrophic split, it was all over there for Labor until 1982.

In Victorian Labor, the VSP types were mostly tolerated, championed by many, a strand of opinion, principled, interesting, and mostly non-sectarian, a voice generally regarded as worthy of consideration by the wider movement.

Fruits of Scullin's tireless work in the Victorian western district came in 1910, when he stood for the Federal Parliament for the country electorate of Corangamite. This was the first election after the 1909 'fusion' of the non-Labor parties, Deakin's Protectionists and Reid's Anti-Socialists, into the Commonwealth Liberal Party. Scullin was backed by a strong local organisation, "perhaps the finest committee that ever supported a Parliamentary candidate in any constituency,"[61] according to an excited report. Another boasted:

> Scullin's candidature in Corangamite continues to boom, he has spoken at Skipton, Lintons, Cape Clear, Staffordshire Reef, Berringa, Piggoreet. Italians [a place], Rokewood, Foxhow and Cressy. A jubilant note is sounded in all the reports of his meetings. Mr. Scullin has been splendidly received at every place visited. He has dealt with Defence, White Australia, and Immigration, showing how they all depend on the land question, and condemned the proposal to borrow for defence, and tax the workers to pay the interest. "To ask the workers to do the fighting and pay the cost too was as unfair as to ask the members of the fire brigade to pay the insurance premiums on the buildings they were saving from the flames."[62]

Winning meant extensive, tireless travel over a vast electorate. Fresh, exciting, and gregarious, Scullin visited the remote fringes along the southern coast, sometimes "riding on horseback to the isolated towns in the Otway Ranges."[63] Another eager reporter estimated:

> Mr. Scullin dwarfs his opponent, Dr. Wilson,[64] the sham Protectionist, in Corangamite. Wherever the two men have spoken, Mr. Scullin's superiority is admitted by the Fusion people. Dr. Wilson has a bad case and presents it ineptly. Mr. Scullin has a good one and explains it to his hearers superbly. His natural gifts stamp him as a coming legislator and are very apparent to all whom he meets. He has held meetings at Mortlake, Woorndoo, Hexham, Ellerslie, The Sisters, and Framlingham, which have been described as "crowded," "good," and "splendid." Mr. Scullin's opponents have ceased arguing with him.[65]

Some voters felted cheated by the metamorphosis of the Deakinites with their merger with former conservative opponents.[66] In 1910, Scullin won with 54.7 per cent of the vote, part of the landslide that elected Andrew Fisher as Prime Minister, with a Labor majority in the House of Representatives and the Senate. Fisher had earlier been prime minister in a minority government for 221 days in 1908-1909. An assessment made of Scullin in 1929 could soon also be said of the new MP: "There is no more thorough debater in Parliament than, 'Jimmy' Scullin. He works with facts, and he marshals his facts in sequence, presenting them with the clarity of a teacher. Always he is logical, and that is why both sides of the House always listen to him with respectful attention…"[67]

At the 1913 national elections, however, Fisher lost his majority by one seat. Scullin was defeated in Corangamite. Joseph Cook, who had once led the colonial NSW Labor Party, and defected to the conservatives in 1894, became prime minster in 1913.[68] In that election, Scullin scored 47.8 per cent of the valid vote, a respectable result. Scullin decided not to renominate for the seat in the September 1914 election fought in the first month after the declaration of war, when Fisher and Labor returned to government, but Labor again lost Corangamite.

Regrettably, said a local Labor organiser in 1914, Scullin would not run again for his old seat.

> Mr Scullin … intends to stick to the *Echo* during the campaign. General regret, says Mr. Macdermid [Labor Organising Secretary for Corangamite],

> is expressed throughout …but it is felt that Mr. Scullin is doing good work for the Labor cause as manager of the *Echo*, which, it is admitted, has become a fighting force in politics. Nominations will shortly be called for those willing to contest Corangamite in the Labor interests.[69]

Only in 1922 did Scullin once more become an MP when, on the death of Labor Leader Frank Tudor,[70] he won a by-election to become MHR for Yarra.

Scullin was comfortable at home in Ballarat in journalism. He took over editorship of the *Ballarat Echo*. The local branch of the AWU bought a controlling stake in the paper,[71] in the city where the union was headquartered.[72] As managing editor, Scullin spread "the gospel of Labor and prepar[ed] himself for the day on which he would re-enter the Federal Parliament."[73] He saw himself as an advocate for new protectionist policies,[74] tariff walls to protect employers and workers, with the social bargain requiring the employer to pay 'fair wages'.[75]

Within some Catholic circles, Scullin came under attack for not doing enough within the Labor Party in support of funding for Catholic schools. For example, an editorial in 1916 in the Melbourne Catholic press condemned Scullin, citing a recent letter of explanation by him which supposedly revealed "that he is no better able to grasp the principles which underlie the Catholic claims than is the Rev. Joseph Nicholson."[76] Nicholson was a tub-thumping, anti-Papist, Protestant pastor of his time. The article went on to say, "the fact will remain that of him and his Catholic supporters it must be said that, when the crucial time came to weigh them in the balance, they were found sadly wanting."[77] Those comments were obviously harsh, hurtful and motivated by a Catholic ginger group, the Catholic Federation, which wanted to pressure candidates of all parties to address the grievances of Catholic parents that they paid 'twice' for the education of children. Once through their taxes and again through fees to parochial schools.

Avoiding sectarian tension was beside the point, thundered the Melbourne Catholic *Advocate*'s editorial writer, as if that could be an excuse for Scullin's ducking the question: "…to say that he put the Catholic education claims on the same plane as the Orange [i.e., Protestant] demand for the inspection of convents or the Scripture Campaigners' demands [was ridiculous]. He cited the attitude of the Labor Party towards these questions to show how it had steadfastly refused to allow subjects of religious controversy to become part of the platform,"[78] the implication being that Scullin was refusing to stand up and be counted. Years later, Scullin remarked that "Catholic papers are very cruel to Catholics."[79]

For another of Catholic Melbourne's newspapers, *The Tribune*, Scullin wrote a long letter in his defence, which explained that the achievement of social justice and Catholic education aims were intricately linked to the objectives of Labor in politics:

> Catholics, on the [Victorian state] Education Referendum in 1904, in obedience to their religious conscience, voted 'Yes' for the maintenance of the

> secular system "as at present," but voting "Yes" today they would be dubbed by the *Tribune* and the *Advocate* as "traitors to the Catholic cause." What change has come over the scene? Mr. Brennan[80] explains that three years ago "the Catholic Federation had only been organised a month or two and had not formulated an education policy." Did the religious phase of the Catholic educational injustice commence only with the Catholic Federation, and after the Warrenheip by-election in 1913, and not 40 years before? During all those years Liberal governments held sway. Does Catholic conscience, after all, proceed not from the Church Apostolic, but is something mundane and accidental, which begins and ends, and ebbs and flows, with the political tides of political parties? …The *Tribune* oppressed by its religious-financial dictum, says: "Some Catholic parents send their children to State schools because in their poverty they are unable to contribute towards the upkeep of Catholic schools …but Mr. Scullin sees no religious significance in such instances."[81]

Scullin then came to explain himself, referencing Catholic social teaching:

> Such instances but enforce on me the necessity of showing a united front to sweaters and food exploiters, who sacrifice the lives of the toilers to their greed. And I take my inspiration, not from the Catholic Federation, but from such as his Holiness Leo XIII, "the great working man's Pope," who solemnly protested that "a small number of very rich men have been able to lay upon the teeming masses of the labouring poor a yoke little better than slavery itself." There is more "religious significance" in the fight the Labor Party is waging to remove the "yoke" off the "teeming masses,"

and so enable them to maintain their families, churches, and schools, than in merely relieving them of an education tax amounting at most to 4 ½d per head per week.

...I have applied my mind long and earnestly to the examination of social and industrial problems, and their relation one to another; and so I am in the Labor movement. I am with those who will loyally help to forge the political instrument strong enough to sever all yokes.[82]

It is not that Scullin believed state aid to non-government and Catholic schools was a state, not a Federal government matter. Scullin thought that wage justice, the creation of a fairer society, the application of the ideals of *Rerum Novarum* would lead Catholic parents to be able to afford and make the sacrifice to send their children to such schools. That was a definitive view forged in an era when Catholic vocations were plentiful, with brothers and nuns, under religious vows of obedience and poverty, deployed cheaply in the schools.

In response, the Melbourne Catholic *Tribune* snorted: "Mr. Scullin admits that the Catholic education claim is one which predicates a Catholic religious duty no different to the just treatment of an industrial claim. Why, then, in the name of common sense, should a Catholic worker be required to pay a tax of even 4 ½d. per child, while his non-Catholic fellow-worker goes free?"[83] This debate was never really settled until the 1960s with the Menzies Government funding for science blocks in government and non-government schools and then the 'needs based funding' with the Federal Government funding all schools under Whitlam's Minister for Education, Kim Beazley, in the early and mid-1970s.[84]

In 1916 Scullin was a determined opponent of conscription for overseas service in World War One, the issue that badly split Labor, in NSW especially, and nationally. "In Victoria, no significant labour movement figure publicly advocated conscription,"[85] although, fence-sitting minister Senator Edward J. Russell[86] was expelled in September 1916 for not explicitly condemning Hughes' conscription referendum.[87] Russell had had a long period in the labour movement and was a former VSP member. Russell stayed in the Hughes ministry until 27 October, the day before the first conscription referendum. Along with NSW Labor Senator Albert Gardiner,[88] the assistant minister for defence under Hughes, Russell resigned as a minister in protest at Hughes's conduct of the conscription plebiscite. Only a few weeks later, despite his professed opposition to conscription, his expulsion by Victorian Labor was confirmed and Russell defiantly rejoined the Hughes ministry. In contrast, in NSW, Gardiner was allowed to retain his membership of the party. Notwithstanding that the Catholic hierarchy decided to leave the issue of conscription to individual conscience,[89] Scullin wanted to go further. The special national ALP Conference of December 1916 confirmed expulsions of federal MPs who had supported conscription.[90] Scullin moved the fateful resolution.[91]

Thereafter, including Hughes' convincing 1917 election win as the leader of the 'fight the war' Nationalist Party, voters were in no mood to support Labor, a party that had largely disintegrated.[92] To some extent, "Labor's first era of government had ended traumatically with the party crippled electorally and stripped of constructive purpose."[93] Scullin at the 1918 Federal ALP conference supported compulsory military training but by the following year that was reversed, against Scullin's objections.[94]

Socialisation

In 1921, Scullin again came to prominence: first, with respect to Irish troubles and the ultimately successful campaign for Irish independence;[95] secondly, in the lead-up to the national ALP conference in Brisbane that October, where the party adopted as policy the socialisation of industry, production, and exchange. Representing Jack Curtin in Brisbane was R.S. "Bob" Ross.[96] Curtin was unwell and faraway (in Western Australia) and preferred Ross, the crusading, socialist journalist and thinker, pamphleteer, and old colleague from the VSP, to represent him.

Scullin, Curtin, and Ross were at the All Congress of Australian Unions held in June 1921 in Melbourne, where the issues were largely thrashed out. There, the various Labor forces surprisingly united on the socialisation objective. But in Brisbane, at the Labor Party Conference, with Queensland Labor Leader and then Queensland Premier Ted Theodore leading the opposition, the meeting was badly divided. The language used by various protagonists and the meaning of terms, including 'socialisation', is almost lost in the sands of time.

At the conference of union delegates, Edward Fitzgerald "Ted" Russell,[97] the esteemed secretary to the Victorian Agricultural Implement Makers' Society,[98] who led argument in the 1907 Harvester case, moved that "the socialisation of industry, production, and exchange be the objective of the Labor Party." He argued: "The only objective of the Labor Party... was to overthrow the present capitalistic system of production. Unfortunately, they had not made use of the means at their disposal for educating the workers concerning what that objective meant."[99] His strident denunciation of the existing wage system was populated with references to do more than just coining slogans. It was important, Russell urged, for delegates and the movement not only to advocate for principles, but also to train the masses for the responsibilities associated with new policies. Bob Ross, in supporting Russell's motion, predicted the arrival of a bad time, and therefore, he said, it was "the duty of the conference to sound a note of warning, and say what they proposed to do to meet the crash."[100] Ross motioned that: "This Congress was not a gathering where any one section was out to get the scalp of another. We must perfect our machine by making it fit to deal with unemployment..."[101] Arthur Blakeley,[102] MHR, asserted that as there was near unanimous support for the resolution, the only differences were on how best to bring this about. He advocated that to educate the workers "Labor propaganda through Labor newspapers" was required. He proposed the movement raise "between £100,000 and £400,000 to establish Labor dailies where they did not exist, and stabilise those already existing..." Only then "would [it] have done something tangible."[103]

A committee of the Congress was appointed to consider and report on ways and means to give effect to the socialisation objective.[104] Besides Curtin, Ross, and Scullin, the members were: Ted Russell, who despite his torrid rhetoric, had a track record of extracting benefits for union members from the 'system'; AWU official and NSW ALP President William Lambert;[105] the then South Australian Labor activist Alick McCallum;[106] Harry Holland,[107] the socialist radical, NZ Labour MP, then visiting from New Zealand; Queensland Rail union leader Tim Moroney,[108] who was strongly influenced by syndicalist ideas; Victorian former Labor MP, and AWU official, John Barnes, who was an ex-President of the Ballarat PLL;[109] Miners' leader Albert Willis,[110] whose thinking was shaped by ideas from the writings of English socialist theorist G.D.H. Cole;[111] Labor Council of NSW leader Jock Garden, who co-founded the Communist Party of Australia in 1920;[112] and Frank Anstey, MHR, who in 1919 published *Red Europe* which welcomed the "social revolution" in Russia and forecast the universal advance of the "drum-beats of the Armies of Revolution."[113] This was a gathering of the fiery doctrinaire, thoughtful theorists, and pragmatic unionists. Some of those boundaries overlapped.

A few days into the Congress, Scullin submitted the report of the committee to a packed audience.[114] He said: "I want to emphasise that this is the united voice of the committee".[115] That report, and the Congress resolutions, were forwarded for consideration at the national Labor Party Conference in Brisbane. Slightly modified from the Melbourne report, the resolutions in Brisbane were passed, as Arthur Calwell explains: "At the Federal Conference of the Labor Party convened in Brisbane [in 1921], it was agreed by 20 votes to 11 to make socialisation, in the terms defined by the Australian Trade Union Congress, the objective of the Party." Regarding methods, this was adopted:

> Socialisation of industry by:
>
> (a) The constitutional utilisation of industrial and Parliamentary machinery;
>
> (b) The organisation of workers along the lines of industry;
>
> (c) The nationalisation of banking and all principal industries;
>
> (d) The municipalisation of such services as can best be operated in limited areas;
>
> (e) The government of nationalised industries by Boards upon which the workers in the industries and the community shall have representation;
>
> (f) The establishment of an elective Supreme Economic Council by all nationalised industries;
>
> (g) The setting up of Labor research and Labor information bureaux and of Labor educational institutions, in which the workers shall be trained in the management of the nationalised industries.

Among other things, the implications of the Supreme Economic Council and its relation to parliament was unclear. The Blackburn Interpretation, a "declaration of the meaning of the objective" was also approved, adopted by 15 votes to 13, expressed thus:

That the ALP proposes collective ownership for the purpose of preventing exploitation.

Wherever private ownership is a means of exploitation it is opposed by the Party.

That the Party does not seek to abolish private property, even of an instrument of production, where such instrument is utilised by its owner in a socially useful manner without exploitation."[116]

The resolutions adopted in in Brisbane became exceedingly controversial. The meaning of phrases and concepts and divided opinion on their ramifications were complications for Labor activists. Byrne in his interesting discussion on the parallel lives of Curtin and Scullin claims that the latter "was working on a different political temporality in which the present was the domain of the pragmatic, while socialism belonged to the far-distant future."[117] Byrne suggests that Scullin and Curtin had opposing views as to what should be done, the first for radical, more immediate change, the other pragmatic and cautious. There is no evidence for this.

In 1921, Scullin and Ross (and Curtin in Melbourne) supported socialisation. Although the distinction between nationalisation and socialisation has arguably diminished in the hundred years plus since, Scullin and Ross were passionate about what they saw as the difference, even if their meaning eluded the wider public.

Scullin, a devout Catholic, could never countenance Communism, or bureaucratic state control of everything or most things. *Rerum Novarum* explicitly opposed such 'solutions' and so did he. What Scullin and Ross meant by socialisation, 'socialising' decision-making, was a concept of democracy or more democratic organisation of the workplace and of industry. This was consistent with guild socialist and Catholic social theory, as well as sceptical-of-state-socialism ideas, and the Catholic concept of subsidiarity – that decision-making is best delegated to the closest unit of society affected by decision-making. Both Scullin and Ross were opposed to the Soviet model, its drastic curtailing of freedom (and significantly for Scullin, the ruthless, blood-stained suppression of religious practice.) Franklin explains in his book on *Catholic Thought and Catholic Action*: "Mannix, Scullin, Calwell, and Santamaria all adhered to Catholic ideas of social justice," whose meaning was that "ethical theory applies not just to personal morality but to the economic and political organisation of society. Leo XIII's encyclical *Rerum Novarum* laid out a vision of society as a cooperative complex of interest groups constrained by justice."[118]

Scullin's friend, Catholic intellectual Kevin Kelly, explained his position:

> For Scullin, the 1921 socialisation objective was a long-term prescription for healing the cataclysmic difference between Capital and Labor by giving workers in the great industries a real and direct control over the enterprises and industries in which they worked and for resolving disputes between worker-controlled industries... For him it was not nationalisation in the sense that the control of industries was to be vested exclusively

in the political officers of the community, for as he said at the time, "I do not believe the workers will ever make a success of nationalised industry, or of industry controlled by the people collectively, unless they are made responsible themselves"... Scullin never abandoned the view that wholesale nationalisation, without effective workers' participation and control, was really State Capitalism; in other words, that State Socialism was really State Capitalism.[119]

Hilaire Belloc and G.K. Chesterton attempted to forge a distinct Catholic interpretation of social justice, neither Capitalism nor Socialism. Both writers' works were known to Scullin. Chesterton in his 1910 book *What's Wrong with the World* argued for the individual's rights to ownership of private property. In 1912, Belloc published *The Servile State* which was a critique of the usurping tendency of modern capitalism to destroy individual property ownership and associated freedoms, such that the proletariat was forced to work for monopolistic owners of capital. Contrary to the appeal of Fabian and state-socialism, however, Belloc saw a different kind of servility through the workers becoming enslaved by doctrinaire state socialism and bureaucratic control. This thinking was highly influential in Catholic and Anglo-Catholic circles, especially in the decades from the 1910s to the 1930s. Distributism or Distributivist[120] ideas matched the Catholic Church concept of subsidiarity[121] that productive assets should be widely owned rather than highly concentrated. In the words of the Oxford English Dictionary, "a central authority should have a subsidiary function, performing only those tasks which cannot be performed at a more local level."[122] Pope Pius XI's 1931 encyclical *Quadragesimo anno* continued and expanded the Church's canvass of the ethical implications of and dangers for human freedom and dignity coming from both communism and unrestrained capitalism, urging the reconstruction of the social order based on the principles of solidarity and subsidiarity. Distributivists sometimes advocated the return of a guild system to help regulate industries to promote moral standards of professional conduct and economic equality and favoured cooperative and mutual banking institutions such as credit unions, building societies and mutual banks. Race Mathews's *Of Labour and Liberty* canvasses these ideas in the context of the evolution of Labor philosophy and policy in Australia, including Scullin's contribution.

In the second decade of the twentieth century, articles in favour of guild socialism appeared in Victoria in *The Socialist*, *Labor Call*, *Ross's Monthly*, the *Fellowship*, and other labour movement-related publications. These were mostly uninfluenced by Catholic social theory, but in their critique of society, of "wage slavery", there were overlaps and parallels.[123] In 1920, Bob Ross wrote an interesting pamphlet, *Revolution in Russia and Australia*,[124] on whether the Russian model had any applicability to Australia. He argued that Australia needed to find its own, peaceful way to the socialist commonwealth and that Russian methods were not applicable to or appealing for Australians.[125] Ross was engaged in a battle within Labor, the VSP, and the unions in opposition to communist ideas. He would always see himself on the Labor Left, but contrary to some on that spectrum, he saw the benefit for workers, families, and the wider society of the implementation of Labor reformist policies. He wrote: "The argument on palliatives must be on the facts… palliation can be progressive – from stage to stage – and thus a process bringing so much of amelioration as to accelerate the appetite for emancipation."[126] He repudiated the polarising falsity of drastic remedies in contrast to "mere reformism".

Ideas of guild socialism flourished in the United Kingdom in the period between the beginning of the Great War to the early 1920s. Some of those ideas were transmitted to Australia. Bob Ross's *Ross's Monthly* did so. Albert Willis, UK migrant (landed in Australia in 1911) and Miners' Federation Secretary from 1916-25, secretary of the council of action established by the Melbourne Congress in 1921, NSW ALP President 1923-35, was also influenced. The guild socialists had a critique and solution for the problems of the day. They were better at expressing their perspective on what was wrong compared to what to do. Primarily promoted by English and Scottish adherents, they were mostly horrified by the regimentation and state-socialist model of the Fabians (and after 1917, the Bolsheviks). They pursued the quest for unions, like the (imagined) guilds of old, to become democratic self-governing institutions which would countervail the authority of the state. On their reckoning, unions could be bodies that recruited employees, trained them, and acted as employment agencies to place their members in employment in individual enterprises, including cooperatives. Bob Ross's son, Labor activist and historian Lloyd Ross, argued: "…just as it was a Catholic, J.H. Scullin, and a secularist, R.S. Ross, who united in

1921 for the purpose of producing a new socialisation policy that was intended to be for its day an alternative to Communism on the one hand, and monopolisation on the other, so a unity of all democratic and progressive interests is possible in the years ahead."[127] Like his father, there was a streak of optimistic bias in the younger Ross.

Alas, socialisation, instead of being understood as making work and politics more community-democratic was often read 'down' unsubtly to mean little more than nationalisation. The word 'socialisation' was newly invented, freighted with cloudy meaning, sounding like a cross between socialism and nationalisation. Moreover, references to the means of production, distribution, and exchange, were conflated with the Marx-Engels rallying call as set out in *The Communist Manifesto*, and implemented with barbarity in Soviet Russia, much beyond anything Marx had in mind.

It is hard to recall that prior to the 1917 Bolshevik Putsch, the overthrow of Kerensky's social democrat-liberal alliance in Russia, and the subsequent swamping of the socialist movement with the ideology of state-control (democratic centralism) and associated nostrums – that the socialist movement was a much more diverse, quarrelsome tradition. Ideas of individual rights and claims for liberty competed with ideas of what would be best for the collective good.[128] A point, also applicable to Australia is this: "British socialism was deeply shaped by liberal-pluralist ideas, while Cold War social democracy was defined by its contest with Communism, making industrial relations pluralism and liberal democracy key elements of its constitution." Yet this line of interpretation is long neglected.[129]

On the concept of a Supreme Economic Council, Scullin and Ross separately, but unconvincingly tried to explain what they meant, the former suggesting the Council would be a complement to parliament, "merely the pinnacle of a system of worker control,"[130] a co-ordinating body of industry representatives. The latter[131] did so by reference to G.D.H. Cole's guild socialist *Self Government in Industry* tract.[132] Ross imagined that the Council would defend the independence and integrity of worker organisation in industry, sometimes in competition with, usually complimentary with Parliament. But this begged more questions than they covered. In this period, the Soviets, too, had a Supreme Economic Council.[133] The unappealing menace of the term would not lie down. As Rawson explained, "the whole purpose and role of the Council was ambiguous, which made it easier for those who wished to see it as a distinctively Communist proposal to do so."[134] The confusion seemed to favour the point Theodore made in Brisbane that it "was very essential, in the interests of the Movement, that they should have an objective that everyone knew the meaning of."[135]

Those things the Catholic Church feared in Communism and doctrinaire, property-depriving socialism, its soulless implementation combined with atheistic, persecuting fervour, were the last thing Scullin had in mind. Kelly argues that "*Rerum Novarum* ... fortified [Scullin] in what as a Catholic … he had long known: that it was the first duty of Government to protect the rights of the poor and that every worker had a right to ownership."[136] Bob Ross thought Australians would never accept communist ideology. They were both in the labour movement, not a debating society. Argument, persuasion, organisation were called for. Commenting on the 1921 socialisation debates, Bob Ross asked rhetorically: "Would you have had the Trades Union Congress commit itself to bloody revolution? Its greatness, I think, was in holding finely and firmly to the view that Australian development, character, common sense, and attainments along the lines of democracy warranted further trust in these proved lines of action."[137] He went on to proffer: "Guild Socialism, I beg to say, in nothing of its philosophy or principles even faintly suggests the holocaust of blood which the critic… sees as inherent in [socialisation]."[138]

The 1921 Conference platform resolution on socialisation, and the failure of the party to explain what it meant, were like bricks in the knapsacks of ALP leaders and the movement generally. The evaporation of guild socialist ideas in Britain,[139] however, and the drift of many of the leading lights in the 1920s to communist and fascist extremes, indicted the movement as faithless to its proposed remedy in opposition to wage slavery. Not for the first time, a political movement floundered in creatively attaching remedies to a diagnosis. Not that guild socialism was the prevailing ideology in the Australian labour movement in 1921. The elite autodidact intellectuals, Curtin, Ross, and Scullin knew its tenets. They wanted to take a lusty swipe at the scourges of modern civilisation. But they knew better than to think the world could start again from scratch. There were traditions to protect, which they sometimes distilled as "Australian solutions". They were in competition with syndicalist ideas, the International Workers of the World-inspired overthrow-of-the-state extremism, as well as communism.

The penetration of Communist Party members and sympathisers into the wider Australian labour movement, especially some of the big unions in manufacturing, transport, and mining, as well as the rise of communist sympathies among intellectuals, complicated the picture. Fabian ideas too, and vague notions of state enterprise percolated through the movement. The truth is that the statement of methods adopted at the 1921 Brisbane ALP Conference, and earlier in June at the Melbourne union congress, was a hodgepodge of competing and incompatible ideas. The concepts did not 'hang' together well. Indeed, the self-contradictory aspects of Labor thinking on socialism have persistently bedevilled its supporters and leaders.[140]

A more modest statement of principle was adopted at the 1927 Federal ALP Conference held Canberra. With respect to methods, now called principles of action, this was adopted:

> Socialisation of industry by:
>
> (a) The constitutional utilisation of the Federal, State and Municipal Government Parliamentary and administrative machinery.
>
> (b) The extension of the scope and powers of the

> Commonwealth Bank until complete control of banking is in the hands of the people.
>
> (c) The organisation and establishment of co-operative activities in which the workers and other producers shall be trained in the management, responsibility, and control of industry.
>
> (d) The cultivation of Labor ideals and principles and the development of the spirit of social service.
>
> (e) The setting-up of Labor research and Labor information bureaux, and Labor educational institutions.
>
> (f) Progressive enactment of reform, as defined in the Labor platform as set out hereunder.[141]

Dryly, Calwell noted: "A comparison of the decisions of the Brisbane (1921) conference and the Canberra (1927) conference shows that the influence of the revolutionary years of 1917-19 in Europe had weakened by 1927, and that the Labor Party was committed to a much more evolutionary scheme for the realisation of its aims."[142] Beazley was caustic in his reckoning:

> Scullin's brilliant and impractical idea of a "Supreme Economic Council," to run the economy while Parliament ran other things, was a millstone around [Labor Leader Andrew] Charlton's neck. Inflicted on the platform by Scullin in 1921, it was removed by [Queensland Premier] Forgan Smith and [Queensland union leader] J.S. Collings at the conference of 1927. Scullin's own leadership was not burdened with it.[143]

Eventually, the Blackburn Interpretation resolution, narrowly carried in 1921, though scornfully derided at the time at the Labor Party Conference as non-binding (because not part of the Platform, and only an interpretation), was revived as a qualifier of hardline socialism in the depiction of Labor policy. By the mid-1940s the utopian tinge of 'socialisation' had lost its brilliant hue. Even so, Australian Catholic theorist Fr. James Murtagh argued then that "Socialisation, today, is a broader and deeper concept than State ownership of certain forms of property. It is a process by which individuals and groups learn to work together… it seeks organic socialisation of the people, for the people, by the people and should be the aim and ideal of all true citizens, who seek national harmony and social justice."[144] This was another attempt to harmonise and give approval to the idea that Labor and Catholic social theory were compatible. In 1948, when Brian Doyle, editor of the Sydney *Catholic Weekly* argued that Catholics could not support the Labor Party in conscience because of its socialist objective, Doyle did not pause to consider the irony as to how much its presence was due to the most devoutly Catholic of Labor's Leaders. Mark Hudson's review in a Melbourne Catholic newspaper of Murtagh's *Democracy in Australia* praised the book for "…blazing a trail through Australia's sociopolitical backwoods for the orthodox Christian worker and the theistic socialist. The book vindicates organic socialisation in the sense in which Christian thinkers like James Henry Scullin and Frank Brennan have understood it."[145] It was reference to ideals now rechannelled into Chifley's post-war reconstruction agenda.

Scullin was in the thick of all those discussions on party principles and policy. He approached the issues from a radical, anti-communist perspective. Lloyd Ross insisted: "The traditional Catholic reconciliation between the policies of the Australian working class and the doctrine of the Catholic Church is made by distinguishing different types of socialism, and in seeing the socialist movement as a conflict against those social ills, which the Church itself has denounced."[146] Yet Scullin's contribution to such evaluation is dismissed in several ways. First, there was the notion that by the end of the decade his socialist proclivities had diminished. Molony insists: "Emotional rather than intellectual, idealistic more than practical, his commitment to socialism gradually diminished and was virtually extinct by 1929, prompted by his increasing concern at developments in Soviet Russia."[147] Second, it was argued that Scullin was not sincere. Byrne asks whether the labour movement's commitment to socialisation might have been deeper and more effective if Curtin had attended the 1921 Brisbane Conference. This ignores that Curtin was represented by Bob Ross.[148] Byrne descends to incoherence in asking: "Would [Curtin] have stymied the act of definition, the subtle reinterpretation through which Scullin reset the objective as a hazy aim?"[149]

The union Congress in June, its definition of methods of implementation, and the wording adopted in Brisbane in October 1921 were little different. Curtin, Ross, and Scullin were intimately involved in the June 1921 draft, Ross and Scullin in Brisbane. Related to Byrne's assessment was that the AWU leadership were determined to whittle down any commitment to socialism or socialisation.[150] But that is a straw-man argument to portray Scullin as the calculating pragmatist versus the socialist idealist John Curtin. Scullin believed in what he said and did. There is no plausible contrary evidence.

Labor's Leader in the Commonwealth

After election as MHR for Yarra in 1922, in Parliament and in his campaigning for candidates, Scullin was seen by supporters as an effective MP and advocate. In 1923, for example, he was described as a thorn in the flesh of the Bruce-Page Government: "He rakes them fore and aft with a withering fire. ...During the discussion on the Imperial Conference agenda he declared that the sure way to burst up the Empire was to drag Australia into every foreign conflagration that British financiers had stocks in."[151] It was also said that: "...he never indulges in hurtful personalities, and he never imputes unworthy motives to a worthy opponent."[152] Hughes, the leader of the Labor rats of 1916, the defectors over the conscription referendum, might have disagreed.

Alert to the interests of farming communities he once represented, Scullin was active in the 1924 debate on the *Land Tax Assessment Act* Amendment Bill: "After a fierce fight ... [led by Scullin] the [Bruce-Page] Government agreed to forgo the retrospective application of the measure, which then passed."[153] It seems fair to observe, in Murray's words, that in the late 1920s, "Scullin was a superb orator in the silvery tradition of the time, exuding sincerity and gentleness of manner, but with a brain that could deftly assess complex material and technical questions, such as taxation."[154] His expertise in this field, his biographer attests, "was valued to the end of his career."[155]

At an election rally in Richmond in October 1924, Scullin "...challenged the opponents of Labor to name one man in the Labor party, who was opposed to law and order. There could be no law and order without justice. The Australian Constitution was founded on Magna Carta.[156] Those who talked about law and order had violated the principles while they were mouthing about constitutionalism."[157] He had in mind Hughes and then Defence Minister Senator Pearce's conduct during World War One.

In 1925 Scullin contested arguments by his conservative opponents that strike action and defiance of orders of the Conciliation and Arbitration Courts explained that unions were lawless, in thrall to foreign ideologies. Scullin insisted: "The Bruce Government was clouding the issue with the cry of Bolshevism. That cry could be counteracted in the city, but it would have to be fought by means of the platform in the country." Because the anti-Labor claims were more potent there, Scullin would be mostly campaigning in regional electorates. "During the campaign Mr. Scullin would be speaking in support of Labor throughout Australia."[158] He was already positioning himself for leadership. As noted above, he was elected Deputy Leader in 1927, and Labor Leader in 1928.

Although winning eight seats for Labor, Scullin lost to Prime Minister Bruce in the November 1928 Federal elections. This was the fifth straight win of the Nationalists, but Scullin's luck was about to change. From 1928, he "revived Labor's hope and faith in its future after a decade of despair in which it had seemed that the party had lost its capacity to evoke a response from the electorate."[159] Scullin's greatest moments in parliament were between his election as Leader in March 1928 and his attainment of the prime ministership. As Leader of the Opposition, Scullin spoke of industrial issues in human terms. Bruce was enraptured by the arguments of his Attorney-General, J.G. Latham, to forego Commonwealth responsibilities for industrial relations apart from a few limited areas (maritime and seafaring, in particular.) This appraisement followed the defeat of the 1926 referendum for Commonwealth industrial powers,[160] which would have dramatically increased Commonwealth powers and responsibilities. Bruce mulled over what he should do.[161] In frustration with some unions refusing to abide by the 'umpire', Bruce embarked on a new approach. He would legislate for the Federal Government to virtually vacate the field of arbitration and leave most matters to the state governments.

This fuelled anxiety for those workers under Federal awards: would wages and conditions need to be renegotiated? How might the transition work? Employer groups as well as unions were alarmed by the potential for unintended consequences. Bruce alienated those who supported him a few years earlier, when he campaigned for more power to the Commonwealth for exclusive industrial power. Now he antagonised them by saying the states should have those powers. He won no kudos from his opponents, and defections among his own MPs followed.

In August 1929 Scullin was stricken with influenza and pleurisy.[162] His absence from the House limited opportunities to flay an increasingly arrogant administration. Perhaps in consequence, the Bruce Government imagined the opposition could be managed. Unchecked, Bruce as well as the Deputy Prime Minister and Country Party Leader Dr Earle Page, committed to a massive change: curtailing the scope of Commonwealth compulsory arbitration legislation. This outraged Hughes, who had "close and highly secret discussions with Theodore,"[163] who from 1929 was Deputy Leader to Scullin of the Parliamentary Labor Party.

The ushering into power of the Scullin Government was the product of drama which followed the disunity of the Bruce-Page Government. Six government MPs, including Hughes, combined to deprive the coalition of their majority. On 10 September 1929, they joined Labor in voting against the *Arbitration Bill*. The Bruce-Page Government lost 34 votes to 35 after Littleton Groom, the Speaker, abstained, thereby bringing down the government. Immediately prior to and in the campaign for the 1929 elections, "Scullin... injected renewed vitality into the party's performance," which projected itself "as the defender of living standards and industrial peace against Bruce's extremism."[164] South Australian Labor Leader, former and future Premier, Lionel Hill,[165] who, along with his whole Cabinet would be expelled from the Labor Party for supporting the Premiers' Plan a few years later, expressed optimism about Scullin's potential on the eve of the October 1929 Federal election: "When he shook hands with me at the railway station at the end of his Adelaide campaign he said, 'Lionel, old chap, I'm very confident over this election. I have never yet spoken publicly in that strain, but if we can't win now, we can have no excuses'."[166] Such buoyant optimism would not last.

Prime Minister

On 20 October 1929, Prime Minister "Scullin's hair was still the healthy, grey-flecked dark of middle life as he proudly …addressed a cheering crowd of 5,000 supporters at Spencer Street station before he left Melbourne for Canberra…"[167] to be sworn in by the Governor-General in Canberra. Thereafter, in Makin's melodramatic line, "Jim Scullin turned almost white overnight with the tremendous worries of this time."[168]

None of the ten Scullin Cabinet members, all elected by the Labor Caucus, had federal ministerial experience although two, Ted Theodore and Joseph Lyons, were former premiers of Queensland and Tasmania respectively. Theodore was appointed Treasurer; Lyons, Postmaster-General and Minister for Works and Railways. As well as the prime ministership, Scullin held External Affairs and Industry. Fellow Victorian Frank Brennan was appointed Attorney-General. Albert Green,[169] the Kalgoorlie-based

MHR, became Minister for Defence. The other five Cabinet Ministers were the pro-protectionist Maribyrnong MHR James Fenton,[170] Trade and Customs; Arthur Blakeley, the MHR for the sprawling NSW electorate of Darling, Home Affairs; another Victorian, Frank Anstey, was appointed Minister for Health, and for Repatriation; MHR for the Hume electorate in regional NSW, Parker Moloney,[171] former teacher, public servant and previous Victorian-based MHR, was Minister for Markets and Transport (divided into two portfolios in April 1930). Also appointed was South Australian-based Senator John Daly,[172] lawyer and Leader of the ALP in the Senate, who became Vice-President of the Executive Council. Several assistant ministers were also appointed, namely, Jack Beasley, the MHR for West Sydney who assisted Scullin in Industry, and Queensland's Frank Forde,[173] who assisted Fenton in Customs. Curtin was not elected by Caucus. Theodore reputedly quipped "one Anstey is enough."[174] Green's inclusion had some satisfaction for Curtin, the latter being the only other Labor MHR from Western Australia at the time. Green in the early 1920s had worked on Curtin's *Westralian Worker* newspaper. He was the senior Labor representative from the state.

In sum, four of the ten Cabinet ministers were Victorian MPs – and one of the NSW representatives, Moloney, who had his home in Melbourne. The only minister native to the jungle of ALP politics in Sydney was a junior minister. Theodore represented a Sydney electorate. But he was an import from Queensland unsure of his footing in the Lang-dominated NSW Labor Party. Because in 1928 the NSW

Labor executive declared that it would "maintain the right of autonomy in all domestic matters," this was playing with fire. MPs from the Sydney Labor machine were unrepresented around the Cabinet table. All the ministers were anti-conscriptionists during World War One. Four were ex-journalists (Scullin, Fenton, Green, Anstey), two were former teachers (Lyons, Moloney), four were former AWU officials (Scullin, Theodore, Forde, Blakeley), two were lawyers (Brennan, Daly). Anstey, Blakeley, Fenton, and Green were the non-Catholics at the top table of the government. (Theodore was ambivalently Catholic, the religion his mother insisted he be brought up in.) All were union members. All but Brennan, Daly, Fenton, Lyons, and Moloney were former trade union officials.

There was no honeymoon for the new administration. Within days of the swearing-in of the new ministry, the October 1929 Wall Street Crash sparked panic. The new government, with only seven of 36 Senators, was hopelessly outnumbered in the upper house. It realised Labor's election program was impossible to implement. As Molony points out: "The reasons behind the downfall of Scullin's government are numerous and complex. But basically, no government can govern unless it has the power to do so."[175] Cornered by the Senate, economic depression, and the Commonwealth Bank, whose Governor, Sir Robert Gibson, was wedded to ideas of financial astringency, the Scullin Government was trapped. Politics passed through a wheel of knives on the way to a void. The imbroglio ahead was pithily summarised by a reporter for *The Newcastle Herald and Miners' Advocate*:

> The continuing background to the events in Canberra in 1930, 1931 and 1932 was the Great Depression. There were daily stories of riots of unemployed and hunger marches in the cities, an incipient Fascist organisation, the New Guard, secretly paraded by night in Sydney, and trade-unionists organised the Workers' Defence Corps to be ready for any demarche from the other side.
>
> The miners' year long strike that produced the Rothbury march and shooting was but one of many dangerous episodes of those days. Political meetings were monster rallies at which the main topic was the cry of the unemployed, the perfidy of the banks and the bondholders, and the indecision of the Labor Government in Canberra.[176]

From the start of his administration, the Rothbury coal miners' strike in NSW severely tested Scullin's team. The situation was at the stage of police batons and high tension.[177] Scullin summoned Bavin, the Nationalist Premier of New South Wales, the coal-owners, and the coalminers' leaders, to a conference. The miners refused any wage reduction. The owners would propose nothing else. The Bavin Government called for volunteers for the mines, protected by police. Lang, injected himself into one of the meetings between Scullin and the miners' union leaders, urging nationalisation. That was the new prime minister's first encounter with the menacing torpedoes of Lang's invective. The striking miners pulled up railway lines, drove away volunteers, and the police opened fire, killing one and injuring others. The miners organised themselves into an army under ex-military miners, to no avail. They capitulated and returned to work on the owners' terms. The Communist press complained in late December 1929 that the Federal "Labor" government, which had promised to open the mines on pre-lockout terms within a fortnight, refused to use the only means that would have enabled it to honour its promise – force against the owners. The Communist *Workers' Weekly* newspaper writer 'explained': "It is a reformist government, unwilling to harass capitalism. Instead, it spent weeks 'seeking a formula'. The only outcome of the secret conspiracy at Canberra was the slave agreement whose acceptance by the miners' leaders has caused Mr. Scullin such 'relief'."[178] The Communist leadership had been replaced that year by a visiting Comintern agent and thereafter operated according to the dictums of 'third period' analysis.[179] A propaganda war was waged between CPA members, their supporters, including acolytes in unions, against the Labor government.

Before the financial markets' carnage on Wall Street in October 1929, Australia was already facing severe economic challenges. In the decade of the 1920s, Australia enjoyed a surge in imports, allied with healthy capital inflows. Thereafter came an inverted story of a famine of imports and capital outflow from Australia.[180] In Opposition, Scullin warned that borrowings to facilitate the Bruce-Page Government's mantra of "men, money, and markets" posed risks for the next economic downturn. Australia's exports were predominantly wool, wheat, hides, metals, dairy and fruit produce, while her imports, mostly manufactures, were drawn from Britain. About 40 per cent of Australia's exports consisted of wool, while wheat made up another 20 per cent.[181] The overseas debt of Australian governments by June 1929 stood at £631 million. Capital was sunk into public utilities and infrastructure necessary for the expansion of primary and secondary industries. Since 1919, foreign debt had grown by 73 per cent, with the most rapid build-up in the late 1920s, averaging £47 million per annum.[182]

Throughout the 1920s, the City of London financiers and the English press were alarmed at the scale of Australian borrowing. By 1927, two-thirds of Australia's capital borrowings were undertaken for the purpose of economic development in the form of public works.[183] Warnings about unproductive ventures were unheeded. There were some "...cutbacks to public sector projects due to disillusionment with the benefit of rural development programs."[184] Bad news in 1929 came thick and fast, well before the Wall Street Crash. By then, export prices had already plunged 30 per cent – equivalent to a 9 per cent fall in real gross domestic product (GDP) – while investors began to sell Australian securities on the London market, making it more difficult for Australia to raise capital. In 1928, Sydney University Economics Professor R.C. Mills argued that Australia needed not "less borrowing but wiser spending".[185] In January that year, "a Commonwealth Government flotation of £8m was poorly received in London, over 80 percent being left in the hands of the underwriters."[186]

Scullin's prophecies came to haunt the prophet, as his predictions came to pass quickly after he became prime minister. Although his government was "elected on the promise that they would shelter the living standards of the working man from the economic blizzard,"[187] this proved impossible. The cessation of borrowing sent a huge deflationary impulse through the Australian economy.[188] Excessive borrowings led to a high level of Australia's overseas debt. With interest rates climbing in response to economic uncertainty, overseas loan repayments shot up. Compounding Australia's predicament was the collapse of wool and wheat export prices.

This passage conveys the state of the Australian economy as the Scullin Government was sworn into office:

> In 1929, Australia was basically a small, open economy specialising in exporting primary goods within the British imperial trading circuit. Nearly 50 per cent of Australia's exports went to Britain... Economists estimated that roughly 25 per cent of Australia's national income was generated by exports with another 25 per cent from tariff-protected industries. The other half of national income was generated by sheltered industries. These ratios changed with the attendant structural change that ensued in the 1930s. Australia's role in the imperial circuit was to absorb British capital and migrants recruited for ambitious rural development schemes, which would, in turn, generate exports to the mother country.[189]

The Scullin Government's initial reaction to the crisis was conservatively cautious: increases in some taxes, abandoning the gold standard, ending assisted immigration, and significantly increasing import tariffs. Compulsory military training was ended as an economy measure.[190]

Australian economic policy was not entirely within the Australian government's ambit. Four extra-parliamentary agencies – the Arbitration Court, the Tariff Board, the Commonwealth Bank, and the Australian Loan Council – exercised a "quadripartite control of industrial and financial circumstances."[191] Before any negotiations with the Commonwealth Bank could commence on refinancing options, the Chairman of the Bank Board, Sir Robert Gibson, informed Scullin that the borrowing of overseas funds could no longer be sustained. He would veto any further floating of Treasury bills until commitments were given towards achieving budgetary equilibrium.[192] Alas, throughout "the 1930s... Australia had an underdeveloped money market and an immature central bank presiding over the country's financial affairs."[193]

In 1930, the Scullin Government sought extended credit from the Commonwealth Bank to pay for loan repayments and increased social spending, mainly for employment relief projects. Responsibility for and control of monetary policy, however, was in contest, with the Bank Governor and his board resistant to entreaties from the government. The Board enjoyed a high level of autonomy. In 1924, amendments to the *Commonwealth Bank Act* awarded control to a board of eight directors, including *ex officio* the Governor and the Secretary to the Treasury.[194] Gibson "made it clear that as chairman of the Bank Board he considered himself loftily independent of the elected government..."[195] Bizarrely, Gibson's term was extended in June 1930.[196] Beazley once asked Scullin why he did so and was told "Gibson's appointment was essential to restore 'confidence'." Yet Beazley wrote: "High officers in the Commonwealth Bank regarded Gibson as quite ignorant of creative banking, and the appointment had no appreciable effect in increasing confidence — since it renewed conflict between bank and Government...."[197]

The Commonwealth Bank was then both a trading bank, in competition with other lenders, and the Federal Government's principal financial arm, possessed of central banking functions.[198] The Bank was responsible for the administration of monetary and banking policy, as well as exchange control. In 1924, at Labor's national conference, Theodore had successfully proposed a platform amendment that the "Commonwealth Bank ...be developed on the lines of a central reserve bank, while retaining its ordinary and savings bank functions..."[199]

In mid-1930 Scullin took one of the more unwise steps of his career. Although Sir Otto Niemeyer was coming to Australia on behalf of the Bank of England to devise economies for governments, state and Federal, and framing what eventually became the Premiers' Plan for the long-range solution of economic difficulties, Scullin went to England to attend an Imperial Conference and to see if he could restore confidence in Australia in London.

If Scullin's Deputy, Theodore, had been appointed as acting prime minister, some of the troubles that ensued might have been avoided. But Theodore was soon to be lost from view by the waves of troubles caused by questionable conduct nearly a decade earlier regarding the Mungana Mining company. He had already proved controversial with ugly rumours publicised about MPs being offered bribes or monetary incentives to vacate their seats before Theodore won selection and ultimate victory in 1927 in Dalley, a Sydney seat.[200] Theodore voluntarily despatched himself to the back benches, after a Royal Commission in Queensland found against him over his involvement in the Mungana mine scandal. Scullin, packed and ready to go to London, then appointed Fenton as acting Prime Minister, and Lyons as acting Treasurer. This was just before the government could bring down its first budget in July 1930.

The Mungana mining controversy centred on allegations of conflict of interest and corruption with regards to the purchase in 1922 by the Queensland Government of certain mining properties and leases owned by the Mungana Mining company in the Chillagoe-Mungana area, approximately 150km west of Cairns. Theodore was Queensland Labor Premier at the time of the sale, allegedly at an inflated price, and he had a private ownership interest.[201]

For one term, between 1915 and 1957, Queensland had a non-Labor government. On 11 May 1929, the Country and Progressive National Party defeated Labor and Arthur Edward Moore was sworn in as Queensland Premier. He appointed a Royal Commission to investigate the Mungana sale. On 4 July 1930, the Commission reported, stating that Theodore and local Labor MP and Theodore's successor as Queensland Premier, William McCormack, each secretly held 25 per cent ownership of the Mungana company. The Royal Commission found that the two former Labor premiers were guilty of "fraud and dishonesty" and abuse of ministerial position. Theodore immediately resigned as Federal Treasurer. Scullin briefly took over the Treasury portfolio. The Moore Government was content to let the reputations of the former Queensland Labor premiers wither in the court of public opinion. Neither Theodore nor McCormack, however, was charged with any criminal offence. Civil proceedings, however, began on 22 July 1931. A 'not guilty' verdict was handed down on 24 August that year.

The Theodore/Mungana controversy sapped attention from pressing priorities. In the second half of 1930, Theodore was like a wounded beast on the backbenches. Doubt about his honesty hung about like a whiff of purgatory. The Scullin Government was deprived of the services of its ablest member. Boris Schedvin, whose pioneering research did much to aid understanding about Australian politics and the economic debates during the Great Depression, reckoned that Theodore was extremely talented, probably "the most able holder of the Treasury portfolio" in the nation's history. Schedvin worked through the extensive Commonwealth Treasury archives to form this opinion. It was easy to recognise that Theodore knew more about economics than the accountancy-trained heads of Treasury that he had to deal with. Schedvin argues that his view was:

> based more on [Theodore's] understanding, intellect, his imagination and grasp of the wider issues than on any assessment of his legislative record. His imprint [wa]s everywhere evident in Treasury policy papers. Whereas most inter-war Treasurers were content to 'approve' a recommendation or otherwise, Theodore examined

> every clause in detail and commented extensively on any provision that needed alteration or clarification... he found himself in the unique position of having a firmer theoretical and practical grasp of the situation than his senior Treasury officials. His grasp of complex legislation was complete and rapidly attained.[202]

Which is not to say that Theodore's judgement was always right. He too was beset with uncertainty and contradictions in forging a policy position. His record reveals inconsistencies. Before Mungana, Scullin thought of handing over his prime ministership to his able lieutenant. The distractions of the corruption allegations and the dreadful publicity they generated made this impossible. Scullin's fortunes were enmeshed with those of his Deputy.

The Australian predicament on the eve of Niemeyer's visit involved: A collapse in national income, in nominal terms, from about £645 million in 1928/29 to £430 million in 1931/32—a fall of some 34 per cent; the increase in unemployment from 9.3 per cent in 1929 to 25.8 per cent in 1931; a major diminution in state and federal government finances due to falling customs and railway freight revenue; a worsening balance of payments, with the London 'reserve' funds critically low; a deterioration in confidence such that it was feared Australia could no longer raise loans in its own capital market to bridge government deficits and loan servicing costs; and a debt deflation problem with exporters unable to meet their interest payments with their assets, pledged against debts, depreciating rapidly.[203]

In August 1930 Sir Otto Niemeyer,[204] British national of English and German origin, employed by the Bank of England arrived with a delegation of bankers and economists to assess Australia's creditworthiness. They met with Commonwealth and state leaders, the Commonwealth Bank's leadership, other bankers, and university economists. They laid the groundwork for a full-scale political crisis. Confident to the point of cocksureness at a conference in Melbourne, the British delegation announced its preferred remedies. "Niemeyer's method of application of remedial policies, together with his air of superiority... proved mindlessly insensitive to political realities and earned him lasting opprobrium..."[205] For his part, Niemeyer was unimpressed by the Australians: the "personnel all round — political, administrative and banking — is, with rare exceptions, lamentable, a circumstance which is accentuated by the marooning of the Commonwealth Government and administration on a sheep run 200 miles from anywhere."[206] Niemeyer wanted to attack the 'ark of the covenant'—namely, Australia's living standards, which he considered unsustainable.[207] Niemeyer thought that letting the exchange rate depreciate was "dangerous nonsense."[208] He reasoned Australia would then only have to pay more to service its debt as well as for imports. He under-estimated the possibility of import replacement and the consequent dynamic boost in primary industry production that would thereby be cheaper on world markets.

Spending five months overseas, mostly in London, Scullin won modest concessions, including partial reduced interest payments for Australia. He also negotiated with the King to appoint an Australian Governor-General, a first. Scullin's nominee, Sir Isaac Isaacs, was Chief Justice of the High Court of Australia.[209] Before his investiture as a member of the Privy Council in October 1930, Scullin asked a simple question. Why was the oath required of a Roman Catholic different to that of those from Anglican and Protestant denominations? (The answer was slight and unexpected. Sir Maurice Hankey advised the Australian Prime Minister: "the only variation consists of the omission of the words "Civil and Temporal" in the Catholic oath from the phrase 'will assist and defend all Civil and Temporal Jurisdictions, Pre-eminences, and Authority granted to His Majesty' which occurs in the Protestant version.")[210]

Unstable parliamentary support imperilled the Scullin Government throughout 1931. Scullin, however, had one sure, steadfast companion. Canberra residents were accustomed to seeing Sarah and him strolling arm-in-arm through the gardens of the city in the quiet of the evening. Inseparable companions, when the pressure of work was not too heavy, the couple could be found immersed in books and walks.

In January 1931, Scullin arrived home by boat in Fremantle. "While still in the west, a member of his staff commented joyfully on the splendid welcome home he was receiving. 'Yes; but wait a few weeks,' replied the Prime Minister, grimly."[211] As Denning appraised: "no man could have faced a more disheartening homecoming."[212] Scullin considered his options. He believed there were three compelling reasons to stay: his retention of the prime ministership was necessary to maintain Australia's credit abroad; second, he considered only he could reunite the party, unlike any alternative, after he returned to find Labor badly split into warring factions. Scullin estimated that the members of all sections of the party would accept his leadership. Further, he felt a paramount personal responsibility to maintain, until less forbidding times, the arbitration system and other privileges gained by the trade unions and the movement – and he believed he was best positioned to do so.

On his return to Canberra, to the amazement of all the moaners and nail-biters Scullin persuaded Caucus in January 1931 to restore Theodore as Treasurer. Bluntly, Macintyre says: "Bereft of ideas, Scullin turned to Theodore and reinstated him as Treasurer."[213] But the better view is that Scullin thought there was no-one abler for the job. He reckoned that the Queensland Government was 'playing politics' by not charging Theodore with any offence.

When Theodore was reinstated as Treasurer on 29 January 1931, Lyons and Fenton resigned from the government. Green was sworn in as the replacement Postmaster-General and Minister for Works and Railways. Forde succeeded Fenton in the Trade and Customs portfolio; Senator Daly replaced Green as Defence Minister. Lyons and Fenton formed the United Australia Party in a merger with the Nationalists. John Latham stood aside for Lyons who left the government and became Leader of the Opposition. They unsuccessfully moved a vote of no confidence in the government in March 1931.

Conflict with Lang was inevitable, particularly as Scullin presented as a man of constitutional propriety opposed to unilaterally repudiating Australia's debtor obligations. But Lang had a point. Why should the bondholders be shielded from straitened, unexpected, and unprecedented economic circumstances? Was a brief moratorium on paying interest on the London debt markets entirely unreasonable? On an intellectual plane, Lang's scurrilous attacks on English finance stemmed from the economic underworld.[214] There was merit in haircuts all round. Lang's position would have been stronger if he had of argued for a restructuring of loan contracts, such as with extended terms and interest holidays on the then current interest rates. In February 1931, at the Premiers' Conference Lang and Scullin argued about allowing default on loan repayments. Scullin and the government, in contrast, *knew* that the bondholders were doing Australia a favour. The country needed capital to develop. Putting that at risk through reckless repudiation rhetoric effectively meant that future borrowings would incur an extra risk premium added to the charge.

An unsettled question is what difference Theodore could have made to the government's fortunes if he had continued, uninterrupted, in office. Hawkins describes Theodore as "ahead of Keynes in what came to be called Keynesian thinking" in that Theodore supported an expansion of credit to fund public works as an instrument for stimulating depressed national output. He opposed deflationary and anti-growth measures, such as cutbacks in wages and pensions, and other economies.[215] There is debate as to how much Theodore was the radical, fresh-thinking proto-Keynesian. David Clark argues that in his first six months in the job as Federal Treasurer and in his earlier period as Queensland Premier, there was a conservative, fiscal rectitude, 'balance the Budget' mentality.[216] Keynesian ideas on economic policy were most cogently expressed in Keynes' *The General Theory of Employment, Interest and Money* (1936),[217] published well after the collapse of the Scullin Government.

Here is not the place to relitigate the causes and effects of the Great Depression and the consequences for Australia. But a few points are worth noting. The British economist R.G. Hawtrey, far from a follower of Keynesian economics, argued that the central bank authorities across the world through their failure to expand credit and reduce interest rates expeditiously at the outset of the Depression, contributed to its worsening and unprecedented severity. He posited: "...it is only when the vicious cycle of deflation has gained such a hold as to cause a credit deadlock, that the banks find themselves unable to expand credit. That state of things is exceptional – so exceptional that it probably never occurred before 1930."[218]

In contrast to prevailing 'orthodoxies', Theodore advocated an increase in government expenditure, a reduction in interest rates, and the maintenance of nominal wages. Ross Fitzgerald's biography argues that Theodore's thinking owed more to independent economist R.F. Irvine[219] than to Keynes. Arguably Irvine was a precursor of Keynes. Theodore's plan was encased within three bills put before the House of Representatives in February 1931: a rate-of-interest bill; a Fiduciary Notes Bill; and a bill to amend the Commonwealth Bank Act with respect to the note issue.[220] Theodore wanted a board, separate from the Commonwealth Bank Board, to make recommendations to the Treasurer concerning bank interest rates. The second authorised the issue of £18 million of public works expenditure facilitated, in part, by the third bill by relaxing the note issue regulations of the Commonwealth Bank.[221] The highpoint of Theodore's expostulation was a virtuoso performance in Parliament in March 1931 defending his position by citing the works of Keynes, J.A. Hobson and Gustav Cassel, all of whom were in favour of reflation rather than expenditure and wage cuts.[222]

In February 1931, the Commonwealth Arbitration Court reduced the basic wage by 10 per cent. Ironically, consumer prices soon dropped by a similar amount, cancelling the intended effect to cut *real* wages. The exchange rate was deliberately devalued in 1931, assisting Australian exporters (product was cheaper on offshore markets, stimulating demand.) Watching such developments was the 'belt-and-braces' Sir Robert Gibson. Also, in February 1931, he formally wrote to the government insisting that the Commonwealth Bank would cooperate if wages, pensions, and social benefits were reduced. In April 1931, he told Theodore that the Commonwealth Bank would provide no further assistance to the government, leaving it no choice but to resign, default or agree to the deflationary Premiers' Plan.[223] A shocked Scullin and Theodore reluctantly opted for the last and battled to convince a majority in caucus only winning over Labor's national executive by 7 votes to 5.

The Premiers' Plan was adopted in June 1931,[224] and the July 1931 Federal Budget confirmed and continued its implementation. Increased sales tax, cuts to public service salaries, reductions in maternity allowances and pensions, were part of what the government did. A big drop in direct tax collections following lower import duties receipts (fewer products were being imported) was part of the package.

Unenthusiastic at first, Theodore in his Budget speech rallied, calling the budget "a policy of internal financial rehabilitation which, though drastic in its incidence, is at any rate equitable in its effects on the various sections of the community."[225] Scullin concurred with this plan to balance the budget without additional overseas borrowing by reducing government expenditure and cutting wages. This meant widespread economies, reducing social welfare programs, and a sweeping review of defence policy – another area where further expenditure reductions were pursued.

Within Caucus, Anstey and Blakeley denounced the 'cuts', drawing moral support from other Caucus members, as well as from the trade union movement especially, who opposed the 'anti-Labor' plan. Anstey favoured the Langite position to repudiate debts. Caucus was restless and unimpressed by the new remedies. Lang, who defeated Bavin in a landslide in the NSW state election of October 1930, was an implacable enemy of the Scullin Government.

In March 1931, at a by-election for the federal seat of East Sydney, the sole Labor candidate and Lang supporter Eddie Ward won convincingly, notwithstanding a negative 14 per cent swing. It was the last election contested federally by the Nationalist Party before it was dissolved to be replaced by the UAP. The Labor Party caucus split, however, when Scullin refused Ward permission to join. On 12 March led by Beasley, six 'Lang Labor' defectors walked-out, and then held the balance of power in the House of Representatives. From NSW, Lang now led a separate 'Lang Labor' party that operated nationally from its base in NSW.

When in March 1931, Scullin could not get Cabinet agreement to reduce pension payments, Gibson refused the government credit. The Senate blocked Theodore's attempt at a special note issue for social welfare funding – after inviting Gibson to address the bar of the Senate on 6 May 1931. Scullin announced a third special Premiers' Conference would be held where further strategies would be devised.

After a Cabinet spill in March 1931, a vote by Caucus members saw Anstey toppled from the ministry. From those elected, Scullin appointed John McNeill as Health and Repatriation minister.[226] Married to Scullin's sister, Catherine, he was an MHR for a regional Victorian electorate and an ex and future AWU official. As the new Minister for Defence, Ben Chifley was brought into Cabinet.

As Vice-President of the Executive Council, Senator John Barnes,[227] Victorian Labor Senator and national president of the AWU, replaced Daly.

Four new assistant ministers were sworn-in: Charles Culley,[228] ex-union radical and MHR from Hobart as assistant minister for Transport and War Service Homes; Lou Cunningham[229] from the NSW regional electorate of Gwydir, fiercely loyal to Scullin and anti-Lang, Australia's heaviest minister, 'the Goonoowigall Giant', as he was known; NSW Senator John Dooley,[230] then an AWU-sponsored anti-Langite politician; and Victorian Jack Holloway,[231] the former general secretary and president of the Victorian Trades Hall Council, who defeated Bruce in the Flinders seat in 1929, as assistant Minister for Industry. Of those, Culley resigned on 24 June in protest about the Cabinet's espousal of the Premiers' Plan. So too did Holloway.

Allan Fraser, journalist, no stranger to Labor politics, an anti-Langite who would in a dozen years become a Labor MHR, wrote in May 1931:

> Four months ago, the optimists said, 'Wait till we get Scullin back.' Now they say, 'Wait till we get Scullin out.' When he landed at Fremantle [in 1931], many of his supporters looked to him to march into the party room, place himself at the head of the Right Wing in the battle that was then proceeding there, denounce the wild men, and either force them out or lead out his own followers, as Hughes did in 1916, and appeal to the country. He did not do it. Instead, he compromised with the inflationists. He brought back Theodore. He

> let those who had fought his battle while [he was] abroad step out, and he stayed inside.²³²

That was much to the dismay and appalled trepidation of Scullin's many detractors. Scullin was not seriously tempted to defect from Labor. Desperate politically, he saw one important duty: to preserve a national Labor Party as a viable political force. That was in jeopardy during his prime ministership.

At first, the Scullin Government, while agreeing that budgets had to be pruned, exercised a policy of 'passive resistance' to Niemeyer's advice, in the expectation that something would turn up. It was open to more palatable medicine.²³³

Economics Professor Douglas Copland, chief co-ordinator of input by Australian economists about the Plan, sketched in his Alfred Marshall lectures delivered in the University of Cambridge, in October and November 1933, that there was a coherent set of policies which enabled recovery "under the economists' plan",²³⁴ namely: a depreciation of the currency sufficient to restore real income in export industries to 90 per cent of its former level; a reduction in real wages of 10 per cent; a general reduction in real government salaries and wages expenditure of 10 per cent; a super tax of 10 per cent on income from property; an expansionist monetary policy based on the purchase of government securities by the Commonwealth Bank with a view to maintaining the general level of prices; and a proportionate reduction in rentier income derived from securities. But as Copland stated later in the decade, all this led to "constructive deflation"[235] – whatever "constructive" meant. He was oblivious of the need to reflate not deflate a struggling economy.

The Premiers' Plan of June 1931 which received agreement in the Federal Parliament in the same month, with the Opposition voting with the government, was no elixir. Schedvin concluded that not allowing the exchange rate to find its natural and much lower rate for the Australian pound was probably the cardinal policy error of the 1930s.[236] He thought the Premiers' Plan "was not conceived as a means to promote recovery, nor did it in any tangible way."[237] Indeed, the authorities' reluctance to question deflationary policy or contemplate a further devaluation in 1932 proved tragic. Consequently, Australia endured an unemployment rate of 20 per cent for four years,[238] one of the worst unemployment experiences of advanced economies.[239] Only after a further deterioration in the state of the economy, did some of the economists who were co-architects of the Premiers' Plan relax their strictures. Even they saw that the economy needed further stimulus by the end of 1931.[240] By then, the Scullin Government faced the guillotine.

Although Keynes, no less, wrote a short piece for the Melbourne press which praised the Premiers' Plan,[241] he stood apart from most Australian economists, expressing disagreement with nominal wage cuts. Besides, it is not clear if Keynes was abreast of all the details and evolution of the Plan.

Lest my account seems to downplay Scullin's personal decisions which convinced him to adopt what became known as the Premiers' Plan it should be noted Theodore, despite rhetorical flourishes which expressed reservations, counselled his prime minister to support the Plan. Scullin was from March 1930 to January 1931 Federal Treasurer himself, from Theodore's resignation to restoration to the role in January 1931. (Lyons, as noted, was Acting Treasurer when Scullin was overseas.) It was Scullin's decision to reappoint Gibson for a further term as Commonwealth Bank chair in mid-1930. Hawkins notes: "This 'Premiers' Plan', reluctantly supported by Scullin and Theodore, was strongly influenced by Niemeyer and Gibson. By this time unemployment was over 30 per cent."[242] The Plan was proposed by the Scullin Administration, backed by his appointed advisers. It might not have been right, but the Scullin Government was hardly alone in struggling with how best to respond to the Depression.

As for Scullin's oft-noted Catholicism, he wore his religion lightly in public. At the consecration of the Church of Our Lady, Help of Christians in Canberra in 1930, Scullin urged:

> It should be our aim to make Canberra a centre from which there will radiate laws of far-reaching beneficence, adding dignity and worth to the political life of the country. We may hope, too, that the residents of the Capital City will, by courage and faith, exercise a spiritual influence extending to every part of Australia, for good government rests upon spiritual sanctions.[243]

On one occasion, fiercely assailed in a letter from a Catholic priest who argued Scullin's socialistic views conflicted with Catholic teaching, Scullin took his concerns direct to Raheen. There, at his residence, Archbishop Mannix carefully read the letter and then, as the fragments fell to the ground as he tore the paper into pieces, His Grace responded: "Pay no further attention to these critics; go ahead and do your duty."[244]

When the Lang Labor group chose to challenge the Scullin Government and align with the Opposition in passing a 'no confidence' motion on 25 November 1931, the government fell. The Premiers' Plan was deeply unpopular within the labour movement. Lang imagined he could defeat 'Scullin Labor' and win a beachhead of support in the Federal Parliament. The members of Labor Premier Hill's Cabinet were expelled from the ALP South Australian Branch, for supporting the Plan. Ben Chifley was expelled by his old union, the Australian Federated Union of Locomotive Employees, for his support. At the election on 19 December, Labor lost all but 14 seats, and the UAP formed the next government in January 1932.

Scullin did the best he could as he was assailed from within by Lang, a restive ministry, and defections to the UAP. His achievement was not just staying on as leader but keeping what was left of the Party together. After losing the vote of confidence in the House came shattering electoral consequences. For Scullin, his tribulations were compounded by another stint as Opposition Leader. As with Gough Whitlam after December 1975, no one else prominent and worthy would stand for the job. Those who might have made good leaders lost their seats in the landslide defeat — Curtin, Theodore, and Chifley included. Frank Forde was elected Scullin's Deputy in the aftermath.

Opposition Once More

Scullin soldiered on, hating the burden, serving his party as best he could, the humiliated loser, sniping ineffectively against folksy, friendly Joe Lyons, Prime Minister. Another defeat in 1934, with banking industry reform the centrepiece of the campaign, saw nine seats return to Labor, including Curtin's in Fremantle. Chifley again lost Macquarie, centred on Bathurst in regional NSW. Tensions over tariff policy between the UAP and the Country Party never broke out into irreconcilable camps. But a new coalition agreement was required in 1934. Page was again Deputy Prime Minister, this time to Lyons. The Lyons-Page ministry was forced to consider the reprisals from other nations over Australian tariffs. Threatened vetoes of Australian meat and barley by Belgium; the suspended boycott of Australian goods by North England provoked by tariffs against Lancashire cotton; Japan's disposition to look elsewhere for her supplies of wool and wheat; and "prejudices aroused against us in Europe, all combined to abate their eagerness to rear still higher our lunatic tariff-walls,"[245] wrote a correspondent for a WA publication.

Scullin preserved his party, as Whitlam explained: "What often seemed Scullin's hesitancy was in truth his humanity. No man less enjoyed his office, and none passed it on more gracefully. A parliamentary party intact and John Curtin as its leader was Scullin's legacy to Labor and Australia."[246] Until September 1935 when Scullin tendered a letter of resignation, the leadership spot was kept warm for his old friend from Victorian Labor, with whom he had an ambivalent relationship during the Depression years and his prime ministership. Indeed, it is not certain whether Scullin voted for his Deputy, Frank Forde, or Curtin. The latter won by one vote, 11-10.

Andrew Clark, journalist with an historian's grasp of the past, once wrote about Scullin violently interjecting against Curtin at a Caucus meeting. Clark saw this as so fierce as to be typical of the undying hatreds that bedevilled Labor politics and its politicians. Clark claims:

> When Australia was under threat of invasion by the Japanese, wartime Labor Prime Minister John Curtin addressed the ALP Caucus in a special session. Fitting the mood, most members were sombre and respectful. However, Curtin was heckled by the former Depression era Prime Minister, James Scullin. The Scullin onslaught was savage and unrelenting. Curtin, his nerves stretched taut by fatigue and tension, broke down and wept. A fellow MP upbraided Scullin for his behaviour. But the unrepentant Labor veteran responded in words similar to: "He did it to me when I was Prime Minister, so now I'm doing it to him." The Labor Party may have changed in the subsequent half century, but one element remains

the same: it is a party of great haters.[247]

If true, Clark was right to spotlight the moment. But wrong on the implications. If Scullin did make this point, more brutally than he would normally, he was reminding Caucus of how discouraging attacks from your own side could be to morale. I do not believe, however, that Clark's account is true. A search through Trove, the National Library of Australia's search engine covering newspapers and journals, including for the relevant period referred to by Clark, reveals nothing remotely like this story.[248]

Scullin emphasised by his example that undisciplined behaviour had to stop. He would be loyal to the Leader. Scullin was returning to the comradeship that characterised their earlier friendship. After Curtin died, Scullin said "I know, from personal knowledge, that he keenly felt what he described to me as unfair attacks when he was in the midst of some pressing war problem."[249] Lloyd Ross, biographer of Curtin, says of the latter that he "came in contact with the men and women who were to influence permanently his thought and action — Tom Mann, Frank Anstey, R.S. Ross, J.H. Scullin."[250] Curtin and Scullin were first linked by admiration for Mann, their joint battles in opposition to conscription, their common cause on the socialisation objective in 1921.

When Curtin became Labor Leader, NSW was still a mess, with Lang still ensconced as the all-powerful boss of the State Labor Party. The Federal Branch of the Labor Party was weak in comparison. (There were two competing Labor Parties in NSW in the 1930s).[251] The internal political forces that brought Scullin down were still ranged against Curtin. "The unity of Labor is the hope of the world" was a saying Scullin knew from his youth. He knew that the continued disunity of Labor was the hope of conservatives across the nation. Scullin pulled his weight in urging all the factions to get behind Curtin's leadership. He described Curtin as "a leader who fights hard but cleanly," who "never has to withdraw or apologise in Parliament and his party need never apologise for him."[252] Scullin was sincere in his commendation, more loyal than many had been to him. But Scullin had little 'pull' in NSW. The party there had to reform itself, which only happened after more defeats at national (1934, 1937) and NSW state (1932, 1935, 1938) elections.

When Curtin came to office in October 1941, Scullin declined to be considered for a ministry, but he occupied an office in Parliament House in between the PM's office and Chifley's. Scullin was a trusted counsellor. Scullin's greatest contribution to Australian politics was to be friend, sounding board, listener, confidante, the person Labor leaders could turn to. All three came to know the terrifying loneliness of life at the top, where nothing really prepares one for high-pressured decision-making where judgement, experience, assessment of competing claims, crude considerations of constituency interests, and, always, *cui bono?* (who benefits?) interrogation informs imaginative, creative, sometimes unconscious deliberation.

Rising from his sickbed, in December 1942 Scullin attended and spoke at a crucial Caucus meeting which backed Curtin on conscription, against Calwell's efforts in opposition. In his biography of Curtin, John Edwards credits Scullin as critical to the 1943 changes to personal income tax powers being assigned to the Commonwealth, instead of shared with the States: "Once in place, uniform tax remained. Curtin, Chifley, and Scullin, the moving spirits behind the proposal, had initiated the most important expansion of Commonwealth powers since federation."[253] This was a permanent change to the revenues, powers, and responsibilities of the Federal government.

In 1945 a dying Curtin had a visitor in Scullin. He recalled: "I went to Curtin in his illness. I asked him what the doctors said. He said it was heart trouble. I told him that when I was in hospital with heart trouble Fr. Hackett suggested that I might go off suddenly & should be anointed." And like any religious person concerned for the salvation of a soul, especially of a dear friend, Scullin offered to "have everything fixed up. Curtin said: 'God won't be hard'. I could get nothing from him but that."[254] On Curtin's death, Scullin said: he "was my friend over many years. I knew him intimately, and to know him was to love him. He had been a true mate."[255] Scullin was one of the pallbearers at the funeral in July 1945.

Scullin was also mentor to some of the emerging right wing Labor talent in the Victorian ALP and elsewhere. He saw the emergence in the early 1940s of the Catholic Social Studies Movement (CSSM), their deep involvement in the Labor cause, including vital support for the ALP Industrial Groups, formed to give support to Labor candidates seeking to wrest control of those unions which had become Communist controlled or significantly communist influenced. Ballarat boy Kevin Kelly, whom Scullin knew as a toddler, co-founder of the Catholic Campion Society, the *Catholic Worker* newspaper, and influential in the first steps in the formation of the CSSM, was a lifelong friend. Kelly saw Scullin's life as that of a Catholic Laborite whose faith and political convictions were fused as one. Scullin imagined the postwar reconstruction era as offering opportunities for new explorations of the application of Christian and sometimes specifically Catholic ideas about the forging of justice and the extension of human dignity.

Scullin was devotional, private, and non-sectarian. When St. Christopher's Church, Canberra, was consecrated in 1939, the then Prime Minister Menzies referred to his late leader Joe Lyons and Scullin, remarking:

> ...perhaps this is the greatest tribute that I could pay [of both] that capacity for having a quite mind in the midst of trouble, that capacity for seeking out once a week, or once a day, or, if you like, once an hour, some quiet moment in which to escape from problems of the world, and in which to compose themselves for the work that was to come... Mr. Scullin would be the first to tell you that he owes that quality... in a large sense to the inspiration that he has been able to get in the work of his Church."[256]

After relinquishing the ALP leadership, for 14 more years Scullin sat in the House. He saw his banking, wheat stabilisation and currency ideas enacted or administered by the Curtin and Chifley governments. He was an adviser on finance, on taxation, and was wartime chairman of the Press and Censorship Committee. He advocated for the Commonwealth Literary Fund.[257] Widely read, he had "studied Burke, Grattan, Curran, O'Connell, Gavan Duffy and Thomas Mitchell,"[258] and a good selection of Scullin's Australian book collection was shipped to the House of Commons library, which had been damaged in the blitz in World War Two.

The eisteddfod champion might once have imagined policies and programs would be discussed and decided on their merits. He spent enough time in politics to know better. They would be debated, contested, and misrepresented. In politics, the desire for control is usually trumps. Scullin's efforts to understand and respect Lang came to nothing. Unusually trusting, possessed of an unbelievable lack of nastiness, he saw the promise of equality everywhere and determined to make himself equal to the challenge. His career was a vocation of service. His NSW Labor adversary wanted to destroy Theodore, not because Lang had better economic ideas in his head, but because he wanted power and a route to the prime ministership. Theodore was in the way. Scullin too. Lang only stood for Lang and could brook no leadership other than his own.[259]

Scullin died in 1953, his last years in poor health. In 1949, Michael Standish Keon succeeded him as Labor MHR for Yarra. For a time, Keon was spoken of as the possible third leader of the Labor Party to come from that electorate. But Keon was expelled from the ALP in 1955. Thankfully, Scullin did not live to see the third great Labor split, which roiled Labor between 1954-1957, beginning less than a year after he died. Much of what Scullin fought for was damaged, imperilled, and lost in the period thereafter. In the aftermath, anti-Catholic prejudice characterised parts of Victorian Labor. This would not be substantially extinguished until decades later — a story told elsewhere.[260]

The End

In retirement, the Scullins resided at Hawthorn, parishioners of the Immaculate Conception parish. When he was healthy enough, Scullin was a daily communicant; Father James Magan S.J. was a regular visitor. He passed away peacefully at one minute before midnight on Tuesday 28 January 1953. His sorrowing widow said: "He just smiled and died." Described in death as "a man of simple faith and solid, unobtrusive piety,"[261] that aspect of his life was incontrovertible. Twenty years after Scullin died, Lord Casey, formerly employed in London at Australia House when Scullin came to visit in 1930 wrote admiringly: "Scullin was a man of the people, with little or no personal resources, who started life with little more than the most elementary education …He developed an enviable command of words and expression, which, became one of his significant assets."[262] According to then Msgr (later Bishop) Fox, Scullin "often acknowledged that the Encyclical *Rerum Novarum* was the foundation of his subsequent ideas and aspirations with respect to the status of the working man."[263] Lloyd Ross admitted: "There were few who failed to sympathise with him because we of the

Labor movement realised that it was a movement, not an individual, that failed."[264]

Although Scullin's prime ministership was ill-fated, out of it came the systematic re-thinking of financial and banking policy, the changes to tax collection, the initiatives embodied in post-war reconstruction, and the fiscal and policy methods for full employment. Additionally, Scullin established the precedent and right that the Prime Minister's considered recommendation for Governor-General be acceded to by the monarch. Scullin's record provided lessons for the next Labor administration, much as Whitlam did for Hawke and Keating.[265] In part, "Scullin's frustrations were Curtin's achievements."[266] Scullin lived a life of purpose. There was much to admire, achievements too, despite the overshadowing years. There was no disgrace in the public and private life he led.

Scullin was never an insider or at ease with the trappings of high office; he more of an outsider close to power. He demanded of government large things, seeing the enemy as those showing indifference and apathy in the face of injustice. Erected over his grave a tall granite Celtic cross stands.[267] Emblazoned on the stonework are Scullin's words: "Justice and Humanity demand interference whenever the weak are being crushed by the strong."[268] Those words explain his life's work.

ENDNOTES

Author's Note

1. Papers of Kevin Thomas Kelly, MS 289 National Library of Australia (NLA).
2. At the time, Crossman (1907-1974) was in despair of advancement into the UK Shadow Ministry. Then the unexpected death of UK Labour Leader Hugh Gaitskell in early 1963, and the elevation of Wilson to Labour Leader, opened new opportunities for the ambitious backbencher: Richard Crossman, 'Introduction', *The Diaries of a Cabinet Minister, Vol. One. Minister of Housing, 1964-66*, Hamish Hamilton and Jonathan Cape, London, 1975, p. 11.
3. Beazley (1917-2007), the greatest parliamentarian never to have become Prime Minister, in Gough Whitlam's estimate, was an MHR from 1945 to 1977, succeeding Curtin as MP for Fremantle after the latter's death. His period in Canberra briefly overlapped with Scullin, who in his final years in parliament, was often ill and bed ridden.
4. Kim E. Beazley, "Labor's Unluckiest Leader. James Henry Scullin. Part 1", *The Canberra Times*, 22 February 1966., p. 8.
5. Don Aitkin, "Obituary. Scholar Devoted to Social Justice. Donald William Rawson", *The Age*, 15 August 1997., p. C2.
6. John Robertson, *J.H. Scullin*, University of Western Australia Press, Nedlands, 1974
7. Liam Byrne, *Becoming John Curtin and James Scullin. The Making of the Modern Labor Party*, Melbourne University Press, Carlton, 2020.

Introduction

8. Beazley, "Labor's Unluckiest Leader. Part 1", p. 8.
9. A phrase coined by Don Rawson. I heard him say those words in one of our discussions in the mid-1980s, partly relating to his article: Don Rawson, "McKell and Labor Unity", in Michael Easson, (ed), *McKell. The Achievements of Sir William McKell*, Allen & Unwin, Sydney, 1988, pp. 26-49.
10. Theodore Roosevelt's "Citizenship in a Republic", popularly

known as "the man in the arena" speech was given at the Sorbonne in Paris on 23 April 1910. See: William Safire, *Lend Me Your Ears. Great Speeches in History*, W.W. Norton & Company, New York, 1992, pp. 477-482.

11   E.G. Whitlam, Foreword, Irwin Young, *Theodore. His Life & Times*, Alpha Books, Sydney, 1971, p. ix.

12   The term "Peronismo" is deployed in Robert J. Alexander, *The Peron Era. A Record, An Analysis, A Warning*, Victor Gollancz, London, 1952. As this Scullin book was going to press, Jim Franklin suggested the Peron analogy.

13   Cf. Tim Duncan and John Fogarty, *Australia and Argentina. On Parallel Paths*, Melbourne University Press, Carlton, 1986. This classic might have had even greater resonance if Lang succeeded nationally.

14   Bede Nairn, *The 'Big Fella': Jack Lang and the Australian Labor Party, 1891-1949*, Melbourne University Press, Carlton, 1986, p. 316. Clune is even more critical of Lang, see David Clune, *Jack Lang*, Australian Biographical Monographs 15, Connor Court Publishing, Redland Bay, 2022.

15   See Trevor Matthews, "The All for Australia League", *Labour History*, No. 17, 1969, pp. 136-47.

16   On Jack Beasley: Bede Nairn, "Beasley, John Albert (Jack) (1895-1949)", ADB, National Centre of Biography, ANU, https://adb.anu.edu.au/biography/beasley-john-albert-jack-9461/text16641, published first in hardcopy 1993, accessed online 2 April 2024.

17   Peter Cook, The Scullin Government 1929-1932, ANU PhD, 1971, pp. 235-304.

18   Warren Denning, *Caucus Crisis. The Rise & Fall of the Scullin Government*, Hale & Iremonger, Sydney, 1982 (first published 1938), p. 47.

19   Lloyd Ross, "Frank Anstey", manuscript of an unpublished biography, Lloyd Ross Papers MS NLA [probably written in the 1950s].

20   Denning, *Caucus Crisis*, p. 133.

James Scullin

The Evolution of a Labor Activist

21 Kelly's Writings on Scullin Family, Typed up by Kelly Family, "1951: K.T. Kelly's conversation with Mrs. J. Kean (Rose or Rosie Scullin)'" Kevin Kelly Papers, MS 2891, NLA.

22 Ibid., K.T. Kelly's Conversation with Mr and Mrs Jack Collins, and Mr Jim Rodgers, Ballarat, p. 2.

23 Ibid., K.T. Kelly's Conversation with J.H. Scullin.

24 Francis Utting, "Jimmy' Scullin: A Personal Sketch", *The Catholic Press* [Sydney], 26 September 1929, p. 29.

25 Kevin Kelly [Review article], 'James Henry Scullin' [review of John Robertson biography]. *Canberra Historical Society*, 1975, p. 106.

26 The Most Rev. Joseph Basil Roper DD (1888-1964) in 1938 was consecrated Bishop of Toowoomba, which he held until retirement in 1952. Cf. Toowoomba Bishop Relinquishes See, *The Catholic Weekly* [Sydney], 6 November 1952, p. 1.

27 John Molony, *The Worker Question. A New Historical Perspective on Rerum Novarum*, Collins Dove, North Blackburn, 1991, p. 130.

28 John Molony, "James Henry Scullin", Michelle Grattan, (ed), *Australian Prime Ministers*, revised and updated, New Holland, Sydney, 2008, p. 143.

29 Cf. Robertson, *J.H. Scullin*, p. 119.

30 James Franklin, *Catholic Thought and Catholic Action. Scenes from Australian Catholic Life*, Connor Court Publishing, Redland Bay, 2023, p. 183; see also: James Franklin, Gerald O. Nolan, and Michael Gilchrist, T*he Real Archbishop Mannix: From the Sources*, Connor Court Publishing, Ballarat, 2015, pp. 166-167.

31 Lasting for a year, in 1911 Hilaire Belloc founded a weekly newspaper titled *The Eye-Witness*.

32 Edited at various times by Cecil and G.K. Chesterton, *The New Witness* was a British magazine published between 1912 and 1923.

33 Race Mathews, *Of Labor and Liberty. Distributism in Victoria 1891-1966*, Monash University Press, Clayton, 2017, p. 107.

34	Robertson, *J.H. Scullin*, p. 8.
35	Paul Strangio, *Neither Power Nor Glory. 100 Years of Political Labor in Victoria, 1856-1956*, Melbourne University Press, Carlton, 2012, p. 72.
36	Byrne, *Becoming John Curtin and James Scullin*, p. 9.
37	That rival being Mr G.J. Mead. See *Ballarat Star*, 12 November 1906, p. 2.
38	Utting, "'Jimmy' Scullin", p. 29.
39	"Labor Observatory", *Westralian Worker*, 7 December 1906, p. 7.
40	Weston Bate, "Kirton, Joseph William (1861-1935)", ADB, National Centre of Biography, ANU, https://adb.anu.edu.au/biography/kirton-joseph-william-6977/text12123, published first in hardcopy 1983, accessed online 4 April 2024.
41	"Ballarat Election. A Keen Duel", *The Argus* [Melbourne], 7 December 1906, p. 5.
42	Bate, "Kirton, Joseph William (1861-1935)".
43	"The Federal Elections", *The Adelaide Advertiser*, 19 November 1906., p. 5.
44	Peacock was Victorian Premier from 1901-1902. Cf. Alan Gregory, "Peacock, Sir Alexander James (1861-1933)", ADB, National Centre of Biography, ANU, https://adb.anu.edu.au/biography/peacock-sir-alexander-james-7994/text13927, published first in hardcopy 1988, accessed online 4 April 2024.
45	An expression beloved in labour movement newspapers at the time to describe Reid's party. Another was "the Fusees" to describe the Fusionists after 1909, when Deakin's Protectionists and Reid's Free Traders/Anti-Socialists merged to form the Commonwealth Liberal Party.
46	"The Fight for Labor in Victoria", *The Worker* [Wagga Wagga, NSW], 6 January 1906, p. 5.
47	Ibid.
48	L.F. Crisp and B.C. Atkinson, "Ramsay Macdonald, James Scullin and Alfred Deakin at Ballarat. Imperial Standards, 1906", *Australian Journal of Politics and History*, Vol. 17, Issue 1, 1971, pp. 73-81.

49 "Ballarat Electorate. The Declaration of the Poll", *Ballarat Star*, 18 December 1906., p. 5.

50 "Mainly Political", *The Worker* [Wagga Wagga], 10 January 1907., p. 9.

51 Graeme Osborne, "Bennett, Henry Gilbert (1877-1959)", ADB, National Centre of Biography, ANU, https://adb.anu.edu.au/biography/bennett-henry-gilbert-5210/text8769, published first in hardcopy 1979, accessed online 4 April 2024.

52 Frank Bongiorno, *The People's Party. Victorian Labor and the Radical Tradition 1875-1914*, Melbourne University Press, Carlton, 1996, pp. 91-92.

53 *The Ballarat Star*, 26 January 1907, p. 4.

54 Robertson, *J.H. Scullin*, p. 13.

55 "Political Labor Conference. Annual Conference June 4th, 1910", *Labor Call* [Melbourne], 9 June 1910, p. 7.

56 Byrne, *Becoming John Curtin and James Scullin*, p. 45.

57 Bede Nairn, *Civilising Capitalism. The Labor Movement in New South Wales, 1870-1900*, ANU Press, Canberra, 1973, pp. 150-160.

58 Robert E. Dowse, *Left in the Centre: The Independent Labour Party, 1893-1940*, Longmans, London, 1966; Henry Pelling, *The Origins of the Labour Party*, Macmillan, London, 1954.

59 Liam Byrne, "Constructing a Socialist Community: The Victorian Socialist Party, Ritual, Pedagogy, and the Subaltern Counterpublic", *Labour History*, No. 108, May 2015, pp. 103-121

60 D.W. Rawson, *Labor in Vain?*, Longmans, Croydon,, 1966, pp. 12-13.

61 "Election Notes", *Labor Call* [Melbourne], 17 February 1910, p. 10.

62 "Election Notes", *Labor Call*, 3 March 1910. p. 9.

63 Byrne, *Becoming John Curtin and James Scullin*, p. 74.

64 Dr John Gratton-Wilson (1863-1948) was MHR for Corangamite from 1903-1910. See: Obituary, *The Argus* [Melbourne], 19 August 1948, p. 5.

65 "Election Notes", *Labor Call* [Melbourne], 10 March 1910,

    p. 10.

66 Strangio, *Neither Power Nor Glory*, p. 94.

67 Utting, "'Jimmy' Scullin", p. 29.

68 Zachary Gorman, *Joseph Cook* [Australian Biographical Monographs 19], Connor Court Publishing, Redland Bay, 2023.

69 "Events of the Day", The *Evening Echo* [Ballarat], 2 January 1914, p. 2. Unsuccessfully, however, Scullin did stand once more for Corangamite in a byelection in 1918.

70 Janet McCalman, "Tudor, Francis Gwynne (Frank) (1866-1922)", ADB, National Centre of Biography, ANU, https://adb.anu.edu.au/biography/tudor-francis-gwynne-frank-8874/text15583, published first in hardcopy 1990, accessed online 3 April 2024.

71 Byrne, *Becoming John Curtin and James Scullin*, p. 89.

72 Strangio, *Neither Power Nor Glory*, p. 85.

73 Utting, "'Jimmy' Scullin", p. 29.

74 Byrne, *Becoming John Curtin and James Scullin*, p. 80.

75 See Alan Fenna, "Putting the 'Australian Settlement' in Perspective", *Labour History*, No. 102, 2012, pp. 99-118; Mark Hearn, "'Industrial Defence Against the Whole World': Deakinite New Protection as Narrative of Global Modernity", *Journal of Australian Studies*, Vol. 42, No. 3, 2018, pp. 343-356.

76 "Mr Scullin's Apologia", *The Advocate* [Melbourne], 13 May 1916, p. 21. Nicholson (1845-1921), sometime superintendent of the Scripture Instruction in Schools Campaign League, was a Methodist clergyman notorious for anti-Catholic tirades. Cf. Rev. J. Nicholson, *The Reporter* [Box Hill, Victoria], 6 May 1921, p. 3.

77 "Mr Scullin's Apologia", p. 21.

78 "Prominent Topics: Mr Scullin's Rejoinder", *The Advocate* [Melbourne], 20 May 1916, p. 22.

79 Kelly's Writings on Scullin Family, Typed up by Kelly Family, 15.7.1950 "K.T. Kelly's Conversation with J.H. Scullin", Kevin Kelly Papers, MS 2891, NLA.

80 Thomas Cornelius Brennan (1866-1944), co-founder of the Catholic Federation, was the brother of Scullin's close friend

Francis "Frank" Brennan (1873-1950). The former was conservative, the latter was Labor and Scullin's Attorney-General in his government. Between 1911 and 1921, T.C. Brennan unsuccessfully ran four times as an MLA for the Liberals and the Nationalists. In 1931, however, for the Nationalists, then the UAP, he served in the Senate, attaining ministerial rank under Lyons. He was defeated at the 1937 Senate election.

81   "Catholics and Politicians" [Letter], *Tribune* [Melbourne], 15 June 1916, p. 3. This letter was dated 5 June, though published ten days later. Scullin in his letter references the 'Scripture Referendum' in June 1904 in Victoria. The electorate voted on seperate questions: "in favour of the Education Act remaining secular" and *against* Scripture lessons and certain prayers and hymns being licensed in state schools. See "Scripture Referendum", *The Argus* [Melbourne], 16 June 1904, p.5.

82   "Catholics and Politicians" [Letter].

83   "Catholics and Politicians, Exit Mr Scullin", *Tribune*, 15 June 1916, p. 4.

84   In a vast literature, see: John Warhurst, "Fifty Years Since the 'Goulburn Strike': Catholics and Education Politics", *Journal of the Australian Catholic Historical Society*, Vol. 33, 2012, pp. 72-82; Michael Hogan, *The Catholic Campaign for State Aid: A Study of a Pressure Group Campaign in New South Wales and the Australian Capital Territory, 1950-1972*, Sydney, 1978; Kim E. Beazley, "Needs Based Education", *Father of the House: The Memoirs of Kim E. Beazley*, ReadHowYouWant.com, Limited, 2010, pp. 192-223.

85   Strangio, *Neither Power Nor Glory*, p. 120.

86   Geof Browne, 'Russell, Edward John (1878-1925)", ADB, National Centre of Biography, ANU, https://adb.anu.edu.au/biography/russell-edward-john-8300/text14549, published first in hardcopy 1988, accessed online 17 April 2024.

87   Ibid.

88   Mark Lyons, "Gardiner, Albert (Jupp) (1867-1952)", ADB, National Centre of Biography, ANU, https://adb.anu.edu.au/biography/gardiner-albert-jupp-6275/text10815, published first in hardcopy 1981, accessed online 17 April 2024.

89   Strangio, *Neither Power Nor Glory*, p. 125.

90   Ibid., p. 122.

91   Byrne, *Becoming John Curtin and James Scullin*, pp. 122-123.

92   Strangio, *Neither Power Nor Glory*, p. 123.

93   Ibid., p. 182.

94   Byrne, *Becoming John Curtin and James Scullin*, p. 5.

Socialisation

95   J.H. Scullin, *A Nation's Agony. The Labor View of the Irish Question* [Address delivered in the AWU Hall on May 16th, 1921], Berry, Anderson & Co., Ballarat, 1921.

96   Joy Damousi "Ross, Robert Samuel (1873-1931)", ADB, National Centre of Biography, ANU, https://adb.anu.edu.au/biography/ross-robert-samuel-8274/text14497, published first in hardcopy 1988, accessed online 5 April 2024.

97   Charles Fahey, "Russell, Edward Fitzgerald (1867-1943)", ADB, National Centre of Biography, ANU, https://labouraustralia.anu.edu.au/biography/russell-edward-fitzgerald-13180/text23859, accessed 5 April 2024. E.F. and E.J. Russell were not related.

98   Recorded as a delegate in Melbourne in 1921 from the Implement Makers union, [Report] *All-Australian Trades Union Conference, Held at Trades Hall, Melbourne 21-25 June 1921*, Labor Call Print, Melbourne, 1921, p. 1.

99   "Trades Union Congress. 200 Delegates Present. Scheme to Overthrow the Capitalist. The Worker Must be Educated", *The Mercury* [Hobart], 22 June 1921, p. 5.

100   Ibid.

101   "Labor Congress. Basic Wage Discussed. Federal Action Urged", *The Herald*, 23 June 1921, p. 5.

102   Norma Marshall, "Blakeley, Arthur (1886-1972)", ADB, National Centre of Biography, ANU, https://adb.anu.edu.au/biography/blakeley-arthur-5268/text8879, published first in hardcopy 1979, accessed online 5 April 2024.

103   "Trades Union Congress. 200 Delegates Present" p. 5.

104   "Labor Congress. Basic Wage Discussed", p. 5.

105   Peter Spearritt, "Lambert, William Henry (1881-1928)",

ADB, National Centre of Biography, ANU, https://adb.anu.edu.au/biography/lambert-william-henry-7015/text12199, published first in hardcopy 1983, accessed online 5 April 2024.

106   Wendy Birman, "McCallum, Alexander (Alick) (1877-1937)", ADB, National Centre of Biography, ANU, https://labouraustralia.anu.edu.au/biography/mccallum-alexander-alick-7300/text12661, accessed 5 April 2024.

107   Patrick O'Farrell, "Holland, Henry Edmund (Harry) (1868-1933)", ADB, National Centre of Biography, ANU, https://adb.anu.edu.au/biography/holland-henry-edmund-harry-6708/text11579, published first in hardcopy 1983, accessed online 5 April 2024.

108   Joy Guyatt, "Moroney, Timothy (Tim) (1890-1944)", ADB, National Centre of Biography, ANU, https://labouraustralia.anu.edu.au/biography/moroney-timothy-tim-7657/text13393, accessed 5 April 2024.

109   "Mr John Barnes. Elected President of the Ballarat PLL", *Barrier Miner* [NSW], 29 January 1910, p. 8.

110   Frank Farrell, "Willis, Albert Charles (1876-1954)", ADB, National Centre of Biography, ANU, https://adb.anu.edu.au/biography/willis-albert-charles-9122/text16089, published first in hardcopy 1990, accessed online 5 April 2024.

111   G.D.H. Cole (1889-1959) was never settled in his ideological beliefs, but in this period, he was the leading British theorist of guild socialism, advocating decentralised association and active, participation in decision-making, self-governance in industry, such that the workplace and the community, rather than the state, predominated in the lives of citizens. Cf. Margaret Cole, *The Life of G.D.H. Cole*, Macmillan/St. Martin's, London 1971; A.W. Wright, *G.D.H. Cole and Socialist Democracy*, Oxford University Press, New York, 1979.

112   Bede Nairn, "Garden, John Smith (Jock) (1882-1968)", ADB, National Centre of Biography, ANU, https://adb.anu.edu.au/biography/garden-john-smith-jock-6274/text10811, published first in hardcopy 1981, accessed online 5 April 2024.

113   Ian Turner, "Anstey, Francis George (Frank) (1865-1940)", ADB, National Centre of Biography, ANU, https://adb.

anu.edu.au/biography/anstey-francis-george-frank-5038/text8367, published first in hardcopy 1979, accessed online 5 April 2024.

114 "The Reds of Labor Movement at All Australia Congress. Social Revolution Advocated. Bolshevik Recommendations", *The Daily News* [Perth], 24 June 1921, p. 7.

115 [Report] *All-Australian Trades Union Conference, Held at Trades Hall, Melbourne 21-25 June 1921*, p. 9.

116 Arthur Calwell, "History of the Socialisation Objective of Labor", *Labor Call*, 24 September 1953, p. 5. A shorter version of this essay by Calwell appeared under the title "The Australian Labor Party", *The Australian Political Party System*, Australian Institute of Political Science, Angus and Robertson, Sydney, 1954, pp. 52-83.

117 Byrne, *Becoming John Curtin and James Scullin*, p. 55.

118 Franklin, *Catholic Thought and Catholic Action*, p. 171

119 Quoted in Mathews, *Of Labour and Liberty*, pp. 186-187. The quotes are from an unpublished memoir by Kelly.

120 Both words never 'took' to the English language. Cf. Jay. P. Corrin, *G.K. Chesterton & Hilaire Belloc. The Battle Against Modernity*, Ohio University Press, Athens [Ohio], 1981.

121 For a survey of the idea's development: Thomas Behr, *Social Justice and Subsidiarity: Luigi Taparelli and the Origins of Modern Catholic Social Thought*, Catholic University of American Press, Washington [D.C.], 2019.

122 From the *Oxford English Dictionary* definition.

123 Jeff Lawrence, The Industrial Workers of the World, Guild Socialism and the ALP's Socialisation Objective of 1921: A Study of Some Ideas in the Australian Labour Movement, BA (Hons.) thesis, Department of Government, University of Sydney, 1974, pp. 26-31.

124 R.S. Ross, *Revolution in Russia and Australia*, Ross's Book Service, Melbourne, 1920.

125 Cf. Neville Kirk, *Transnational Radicalism and the Connected Lives of Tom Mann and Robert Samuel Ross*, Liverpool University Press, Liverpool, 2017, p. 158.

126 Ross, *Revolution in Russia and Australia*, pp. 54, 57f. Cited in Kirk, Ibid., p. 156.

127 Lloyd Ross, "Labour, Catholicism and Democratic Socialism", *Twentieth Century, An Australian Quarterly Review*, Vol. 2, No. 2, December 1947, p. 82.

128 Cf. Peter Ackers and Alistair J. Reid (eds), *Alternatives to State-Socialism in Britain: Other Worlds of Labour in the Twentieth Century*, Palgrave Macmillan, 2016.

129 Michael Easson, Review of Ackers and Reid, *Labour History*, No. 114, May 2018, p. 197.

130 Lawrence, p. 38. The words quoted are from Lawrence's summary.

131 R.S. Ross, "The Socialisation of Industry. Why A Supreme Economic Council?", *Ross's Monthly*, Vol. 7, No. 77, 8 April 1922, pp. 4-5.

132 G.D.H. Cole, *Self-Governance in Industry*, G. Bell & Sons, Ltd., London, Fifth Edition Revised, 1920.

133 Samuel A. Oppenheim, "The Supreme Economic Council 1917-21", *Soviet Studies*, Vol. 25, No. 1, July 1973, pp. 3-27.

134 Rawson, *Labor in Vain*, p. 85.

135 Australian Labor Party, *Official Report of Proceedings of the Ninth Commonwealth Conference, October 1921*, Labor Call Print, Melbourne, 1921, p. 6.

136 Kelly [Review article], "James Henry Scullin", p. 106.

137 R.S. Ross, "A Reply" [to an article "Panaceas. v. Revolution: Australian Way"], *Steads Review* (Australian Edition), Vol. 56, No. 5, 3 September 1921, p. 260.

138 Ibid. Both Ross quotes are cited in Michael Easson, "Burke and Australian Labor", in Damien Freeman, editor, *The Market's Morals: Responding to Jesse Norman*, The Kapunda Press, Connor Court Publishing, Redland Bay, 2020.

139 Some of this story is told in Michael Easson, "The Scot Guild Socialists", New Boots from the Old. Matthew Walker Robieson and the Struggle for Guild Socialism, PhD, School of Humanities and the Social Sciences, ADFA at UNSW, 2013, pp. 139-193.

140 D.W. Rawson, "Labour, Socialism and the Working Class", *Australian Journal of Politics and History*, Vol. 7, Issue 1,

May 1961, p. 75.
141 Calwell, "History of the Socialisation Objective of Labor", p. 5.
142 Ibid.
143 Beazley, "Labor's Unluckiest Leader. James Henry Scullin. Part II", *Canberra Times*, 23 February 1966, p. 10.
144 James G. Murtagh, *Democracy in Australia*, Catholic Social Guild, Melbourne, 1946, pp. 59-60. I have eliminated in the quote the alternative 'z' spelling of socialisation.
145 Mark Hudson, Review of James Murtagh, *Democracy in Australia*, *The Advocate* [Melbourne], 28 August 1946, p. 10.
146 Ross, "Labour, Catholicism and Democratic Socialism", p. 77.
147 Molony, "James Henry Scullin", p. 144.
148 Australian Labor Party, *Official Report of Proceedings of the Ninth Commonwealth Conference, October 1921*, Loc. Cit., p. 4.
149 Byrne, *Becoming John Curtin and James Scullin*, p. 55.
150 Ibid., p. 158.

Labor's Leader in the Commonwealth

151 Hitting Hard, *Daily Standard* [Brisbane], 18 August 1923, p 10.
152 Francis Utting, "'Jimmy' Scullin", p. 29.
153 "Cutting Up 60 Million of Your Money", *Westralian Worker*, 20 June 1924. p. 9.
154 Murray, *The Confident Years. Australia in the 1920s*, p. 199.
155 Robertson, *J.H. Scullin*, p. 85.
156 Not to be detained here, it was more complex than what Scullin said. Also relevant were the 1688 Bill of Rights, habeas corpus, common law, US Constitution (federal system, separation of powers) as well as Magna Carta.
157 "Federal Elections. Scullin Scathing", *Richmond Guardian* [Melbourne], 17 October 1925, p. 2.
158 Ibid.
159 By A Staff Reporter, "James Scullin. A Quiet Man Ruled in Troubled Days", *The Newcastle Herald and Miners Advocate*, 30 January 1953, p. 2.
160 See Aaron Wildavsky, "The 1926 Referendum", Aaron

Wildavsky & Dagmar Carboch, eds, *Studies in Australian Politics*, F.W. Cheshire, Melbourne, 1958, pp. 10-12.

161 Geoffrey Sawer, *Australian Federal Politics and Law 1901-1929* Melbourne University Press, Carlton, 1956, pp. 268-270; 276-278.

162 Ross McMullin, *The Light on the Hill. The Australian Labor Party 1891-1991*, Oxford University Press Australia, Oxford, 1991, p. 150.

163 L.F. Fitzhardinge, *William Morris Hughes. A Political Biography. vol. 2: The Little Digger 1914-1952*, Angus & Robertson Publishers, Sydney, 1979, p. 580.

164 Strangio, *Neither Power Nor Glory*, p. 171.

165 Ray Broomhill, "Hill, Lionel Laughton (1881-1963)", ADB, National Centre of Biography, ANU, https://adb.anu.edu.au/biography/hill-lionel-laughton-6671/text11485, published first in hardcopy 1983, accessed online 5 April 2024.

166 Lionel Hill, "Jim Scullin", *The Register News-Pictorial* [Adelaide], 14 October 1929, p. 3.

Prime Minister

167 Robert Murray, *The Confident Years. Australia in the 1920s*, Australian Scholarly, North Melbourne, 2020, p. 227.

168 Norman Makin, *Federal Labour Leaders*, Union Printing Pty. Limited, Sydney, 1961, p. 87.

169 G.C. Bolton, "Green, Albert Ernest (1869-1940)", ADB, National Centre of Biography, ANU, https://adb.anu.edu.au/biography/green-albert-ernest-6468/text11077, published first in hardcopy 1983, accessed online 14 February 2024.

170 J.R. Robertson, "Fenton, James Edward (1864-1950)", ADB, National Centre of Biography, ANU, https://adb.anu.edu.au/biography/fenton-james-edward-6155/text10571, published first in hardcopy 1981, accessed online 31 January 2024.

171 C.J. Lloyd, "Moloney, Parker John (1879-1961)", ADB, National Centre of Biography, ANU, https://adb.anu.edu.au/biography/moloney-parker-john-7617/text13311, published first in hardcopy 1986, accessed online 14 February 2024.

172 Ray Broomhill, "Daly, John Joseph (1891-1942)", ADB,

National Centre of Biography, ANU, https://adb.anu.edu.au/biography/daly-john-joseph-5874/text9993, published first in hardcopy 1981, accessed online 14 February 2024.

173 Neil Lloyd and Malcolm Saunders, "Forde, Francis Michael (Frank) (1890-1983)", ADB, National Centre of Biography, ANU, https://adb.anu.edu.au/biography/forde-francis-michael-frank-12504/text22477, published first in hardcopy 2007, accessed online 14 February 2024.

174 McMullin, *The Light on the Hill*, p. 154. On Theodore's opposition to Curtin joining Cabinet, Denning, *Caucus Crisis*, p. 114.

175 Molony, 'James Henry Scullin', p. 147.

176 By A Staff Reporter, "James Scullin", p. 2.

177 Ibid.

178 "Seeking A Formula", *The Workers' Weekly* [Sydney, publication of the CPA], 6 December 1929, p. 1.

179 In mid-1928 at the Congress of the communist parties from around the world, the Communist International, the Comintern, in Moscow, declared that communists needed to expose social democrats and Laborites as little better than fascists, calling them social fascists. In their nomenclature, the first period was the revolutionary ferment during and after World War I, including the defeat of uprisings in Germany and Hungary in 1919; the second period was the consolidation of capitalism in the 1920s; the third period being the weakening of capitalism and the emerging, consequent opportunity for revolutionary activity. See Kevin McDermott, "Stalin and the Comintern during the 'Third Period', 1928-33", *European History Quarterly,* Vol. 25, No. 3, 1995, pp. 409-429.

180 Alex Millmow, *The Power of Economic Ideas: The Origins of Keynesian Macroeconomic Management in Interwar Australia 1929-39*, ANU ePress, Canberra, 2010, p. 34.

181 Ibid., p. 33.

182 Ibid.

183 R.C. Mills, "Australian Loan Policy", R.C. Mills, P. Campbell and G.V. Portus, (ed), *Studies in Australian Affairs*, Macmillan/Melbourne University Press,

Melbourne, 1928, pp. 112-115.

184 W.A. Sinclair. "External and Internal Influences in the Depression of the 1930s in Australia", *Economics*, Vol. 9, No. 2, September 1974, pp. 55-60.

185 Mills, "Australian Loan Policy", p. 117.

186 Robertson, *J.H. Scullin*, p. 151.

187 Millmow, *The Power of Economic Ideas*, p. 74.

188 C.B. Schedvin, *Australia and the Great Depression*, Sydney University Press, Camperdown, 1970, p. 4.

189 Millmow, *The Power of Economic Ideas*, p. 33.

190 Denning, *Caucus Crisis*, p. 99.

191 N. Brown, *Governing Prosperity*, Cambridge University Press, Melbourne, 1995, p. 51.

192 E.O.G. Shann and D.B. Copland, *The Crisis in Australian Finance 1929 to 1931. Documents on Budgetary and Economic Policy*, Angus & Robertson, Sydney, 1931.

193 Millmow, *The Power of Economic Ideas*, p. 40.

194 For authoritative background see: L.F. Giblin, *The Growth of a Central Bank: The Development of the Commonwealth Bank of Australia, 1924-1945*, Melbourne University Press, Carlton, 1951; and C.B. Schedvin, *In Reserve: Central Banking in Australia, 1945-75*, Macmillan, Sydney, 1992.

195 McMullin, *The Light on the Hill*, p. 155.

196 Cf. Denning, *Caucus Crisis*, p. 109.

197 Beazley, "Labor's Unluckiest Leader. James Henry Scullin. Part I".

198 Only in 1959 were those functions split into the Reserve Bank of Australia and the Commonwealth Banking Corporation.

199 ALP, *Official Report of Proceedings of the Tenth Commonwealth Conference*, 1924, p. 4.

200 Ross Fitzgerald, *"Red Ted". The Life of Theodore Roosevelt*, University of Queensland Press, St Lucia, 1994, pp. 243-276. Theodore was unexpectedly defeated in 1925 when he stood for the Queensland Federal seat of Herbert. He won the Federal seat of Dalley in NSW in a by-election in 1927.

201 K.H. Kennedy, *The Mungana Affair. State Mining and Political Corruption in the 1920s*, University of Queensland

Press, St Lucia, 1978; Fitzgerald, *"Red Ted"*.

202 Schedvin, *Australia and the Great Depression*, p. 119.

203 D.B. Copland, "Australian Policy in Depression", A.D. Gayer, editor, *The Lessons of Monetary Experience: Essays in Honour of Irving Fisher*, 1937, pp. 398-399.

204 Parts of the press, including the Labor press, falsely implied Niemeyer was Jewish. But he was born to an English mother and a German migrant from Hanover. See: Anne Henderson, *Joseph Lyons. The Peoples' Prime Minister*, New South, Sydney, 2011, p. 223.

205 Millmow, *The Power of Economic Ideas*, p. 73.

206 K. Tsokhas, "Sir Otto Niemeyer, the Bankrupt State and the Federal System", *Australian Journal of Political Science*, Vol. 30, 1995, p. 24.

207 Millmow, *The Power of Economic Ideas*, p. 66.

208 Ibid., p. 71.

209 John Waugh, "An Australian in the Palace of the King-Emperor: James Scullin, George V and the Appointment of the First Australian-born Governor-General", *Federal Law Review*, Vol. 39, No. 2, 2011, pp. 235-253; L F Crisp, "The Appointment of Sir Isaac Isaacs as Governor-General of Australia, 1930: J H Scullin's Account of the Buckingham Palace Interviews", *Historical Studies: Australia and New Zealand*, Vol. 11, Issue 42, 1964, pp. 253-257.

210 [Personal Letter] M.P.A. Hankey, Privy Council Office, to Rt. Hon. J.H. Scullin, 27 October 1930, John Scullin Papers, MS 356 NLA.

211 Allan Fraser, "The Scullin Complex. The Man Who Started at the Top. Motives of Plain James", *The Sun* [Sydney], 17 May 1931, p. 3.

212 Denning, *Caucus Crisis*, p. 124.

213 Stuart Macintyre, *The Oxford History of Australia, Vol. 4, 1901-1942*, Oxford University Press, Melbourne, 1986, p. 263.

214 David Clark, "Was Lang Right?", Heather Radi and Peter Spearritt, editors, *Jack Lang*, Hale & Iremonger, Sydney, 1977, pp. 156-157.

215 John Hawkins, "Ted Theodore: The Proto-Keynesian",

Economic Roundup, Issue 1, The Treasury, Canberra, 2010, https://treasury.gov.au/publication/economic-roundup-issue-1-2010/economic-roundup-issue-1-2010.

216   David Clark, "EG Theodore: His Economics and His Influence", *Economics*, Vol. 10, No. 1, March 1975, pp. 27-33.

217   John Maynard Keynes, *The General Theory of Employment, Interest and Money*, Palgrave Macmillan, London, 1936.

218   R.G. Hawtrey, *A Century of the Bank Rate*, Longmans, London, 1938, pp. 270, 273.

219   B.J. McFarlane. "Irvine, Robert Francis (1861-1941)", ADB, National Centre of Biography, ANU, https://adb.anu.edu.au/biography/irvine-robert-francis-6800/text11763, published first in hardcopy 1983, accessed online 11 February 2024.

220   Millmow, *The Power of Economic Ideas*, p. 83.

221   Ibid.

222   K.H. Kennedy, "E.G. Theodore", in R.T. Appleyard and C.B. Schedvin, (eds), *Australian Financiers. Biographical Essays*, Macmillan, South Melbourne, 1988, p. 296.

223   Gibson's letter and Theodore's reply are reproduced in E.O.G. Shann and D.B. Copland, editors, *The Battle of the Plans, Documents Relating to the Premiers' Conference, May 25th to June 11th 1931*, Angus and Robertson Limited, Sydney, 1931, pp. 44-56.

224   Much of my analysis follows John Hawkins on Theodore.

225   Ibid. The quote from Theodore is from House of Representatives, *Hansard*, 10 July 1931, p. 3746.

226   J.R. Robertson, "McNeill, John James (1868-1943)", ADB, National Centre of Biography, ANU, https://adb.anu.edu.au/biography/mcneill-john-james-7434/text12941, published first in hardcopy 1986, accessed online 18 April 2024.

227   Norma Marshall, "Barnes, John (1868-1938)", ADB, National Centre of Biography, ANU, https://adb.anu.edu.au/biography/barnes-john-61/text8597, published first in hardcopy 1979, accessed online 18 April 2024.

228   R.P. Davis, "Culley, Charles Ernest (1877-1949)", ADB, National Centre of Biography, ANU, https://adb.anu.edu.au/biography/culley-charles-ernest-5839/text9921, published

first in hardcopy 1981, accessed online 20 April 2024.

229 Ross McMullin, "Cunningham, Lucien Lawrence (Lou) (1889-1948)", ADB, National Centre of Biography, ANU, https://adb.anu.edu.au/biography/cunningham-lucien-lawrence-lou-9879/text17483, published first in hardcopy 1993, accessed online 20 April 2024.

230 Robin Gollan and Moira Scollay, "Dooley, John Braidwood (1883-1961)", ADB, National Centre of Biography, ANU, https://adb.anu.edu.au/biography/dooley-john-braidwood-6001/text10249, published first in hardcopy 1981, accessed online 20 April 2024.

231 D.P. Blaazer, "Holloway, Edward James (Jack) (1875-1967)", ADB, National Centre of Biography, ANU, https://adb.anu.edu.au/biography/holloway-edward-james-jack-10523/text18677, published first in hardcopy 1996, accessed online 20 April 2024.

232 Allan Fraser, "The Scullin Complex", p. 3.

233 Ibid., pp. 67-8.

234 D.B. Copland, *Australia and the World Crisis 1929-33*, Cambridge University Press, Cambridge, 1934, p. 50.

235 D.B. Copland, "Australian Policy in Depression", A.D. Gayer, editor, *The Lessons of Monetary Experience: Essays in Honour of Irving Fisher*, George Allen & Unwin Ltd., London, 1937.

236 Schedvin, *In Reserve*, pp. 52-53.

237 Schedvin, *Australia and the Great Depression*.

238 Millmow, *The Power of Economic Ideas*, p. 28.

239 Ibid., p. 36.

240 D.B. Copland, *Inflation and Expansion: Essays on the Australian Economy*, Cheshire, Melbourne, 1951, p. 22.

241 "World-Famous Economist Praises Our Efforts. J.M. Keynes Reviews Australia's Position. Tribute to Premier's Plan", *The Herald* [Melbourne], 27 June 1932, p. 1.

242 John Hawkins, "James Scullin. Depression Treasurer", *Economic Roundup*, Issue 2, The Treasury, Canberra, 2010, https://treasury.gov.au/publication/economic-roundup-issue-2-2010/economic-roundup-issue-2-2010/james-scullin-depression-treasurer.

243   *The Angelus*, 6 April 1930.

244   [Typescript notes], Scullin Draft, p. 6. Kevin Kelly Papers, Folder 8, MS 2891, NLA.

Opposition Once More

245   'By Satellite', "Political Notes. Coalition Government Formed", *The Weekly Gazette* [Western Australia], 9 November 1934, p. 7.

246   Whitlam, Foreword, Irwin Young, *Theodore. His Life & Times*, p. x.

247   Andrew Clark, "In the Boots of Lang and Scullin", *Sun Herald*, 14 August 1994. p. 29.

248   John Edwards notes: "There is no date offered in the piece, or suggestion of the issue. I did not use it my book, and I cannot find it in other Curtin or Scullin biographies. It sounds quite unlike the usual manner of Scullin." Email: John Edwards to Michael Easson, 10 May 2024.

249   "Prime Minister's Strenuous Role. Mr Scullin's Views on Unfair Criticisms", *Kalgoorlie Miner* [WA], 14 July 1915, p. 1.

250   Lloyd Ross, "The Education of John Curtin", *The Australian Highway*, Vol. 27, new series, No. 1, 1 August 1945, p. 49.

251   Don Rawson, "McKell and Labor Unity", Loc. Cit.

252   "'Fights Cleanly'. Party Tribute to Mr Curtin", *The Canberra Times*, 9 June 1939, p. 4.

253   John Edwards, *John Curtin's War. Volume II. Triumph and Decline*, Viking, 2018, p. 55.

254   Kelly's Writings on Scullin Family, Typed up by Kelly Family, 15.7.1950 K.T. Kelly's Conversation with J.H. Scullin, Kevin Kelly Papers, MS 2891, NLA.

255   Byrne, *Becoming John Curtin and James Scullin*, p. 3.

256   "The Inner Life of James Henry Scullin. Prime Minister's Tribute", *The Advocate* [Melbourne], 5 February 1953, p. 2.

257   Beazley, "Labor's Unluckiest Leader. James Henry Scullin. Part II", p. 10.

258   Kevin Kelly [Review article], 'James Henry Scullin', pp. 104-105.

259 Cf. David Clune, *Jack Lang*.

260 Cf. Michael Easson, '1954. The Third Great Labor Split', *Tocsin, journal of the John Curtin Research Centre*, Issue 20, Special edition: Labor First in the World: Labor Making Australian History, March 2024, pp. 30-33.

The End

261 "The Inner Life of James Henry Scullin. Prime Minister's Tribute", p. 2.

262 Lord Casey, "The Scullin I Remember", *Sydney Morning Herald*, 18 August 1973, p. 20.

263 "Monsignor Fox's Panegyric", *The Advocate* [Melbourne] 5 February 1953, p. 3.

264 Lloyd Ross, "A Great Leader Has Gone", *The Herald* [Melbourne], 29January 1953, p. 10.

265 Frank Bongiorno, "The Whitlam Legacy for the Fraser and Hawke Governments, Scott Prasser and David Clune, editors, *The Whitlam Era. A Reappraisal of Government, Politics and Policy*, Connor Court, Redland Bay [Queensland], 2022, pp. 445-465.

266 Beazley, "Labor's Unluckiest Leader. James Henry Scullin. Part II", p. 10.

267 Ceremony at Grave of Mr Scullin, *The Argus* [Melbourne], 31 October 1953, p. 4.

268 Robertson, *J.H. Scullin*, p. 479.

www.ingramcontent.com/pod-product-compliance
Lightning Source LLC
Chambersburg PA
CBHW071456160426
43195CB00013B/2133